P9-DXK-093

WITHDRAWN

OCT   2002

JB JACKSON, M.
Orgill, Roxane.
Mahalia : a life in
gospel music /

5 x05

MAHALIA
A Life in Gospel Music

MAHALIA

A Life in Gospel Music

Roxane Orgill

CANDLEWICK PRESS
CAMBRIDGE, MASSACHUSETTS

ALAMEDA FREE LIBRARY
2200-A CENTRAL AVENUE
ALAMEDA CA 94501

Copyright © 2002 by Roxane Orgill

All rights reserved. No part of this book may be reproduced, transmitted,
or stored in an information retrieval system in any form or by
any means, graphic, electronic, or mechanical, including photocopying,
taping, and recording, without prior written permission from the publisher.

First edition 2002

"Move On Up a Little Higher," by Rev. W. Brewster. Copyright © 1946 (Renewed) by
Unichappell Music Inc. All rights reserved. Used by permission of Warner Bros.
Publications U.S. Inc., Miami, FL 33014.

"Precious Lord Take My Hand," by Thomas A. Dorsey. Copyright © 1938 (Renewed)
by Warner-Tamerlane Publishing Corp. All rights outside the U.S.A. controlled by
Unichappell Music Inc. All rights reserved. Used by permission of Warner Bros.
Publications U.S. Inc., Miami, FL 33014.

Library of Congress Cataloging-in-Publication Data

Orgill, Roxane.
Mahalia : a life in gospel music / Roxane Orgill. — 1st ed.
p. cm.
ISBN 0-7636-1011-9
1. Jackson, Mahalia, 1911–1972—Juvenile literature. 2. Gospel musicians—
United States—bibliography—Juvenile literature. [1. Jackson, Mahalia, 1911–1972.
2. Singers. 3. Women—Biography. 4. Afro-Americans—Biography.] I. Title.
ML3930.J2 O74 2002
782.25'4'092—dc21
[B]   00-048669

2 4 6 8 10 9 7 5 3 1

Printed in Hong Kong

This book was typeset in Weiss.

Photo research by Lisa Von Seggern

Jacket calligraphy by Jenna LaReau

Candlewick Press
2067 Massachusetts Avenue
Cambridge, Massachusetts 02140

visit us at www.candlewick.com

For Charlotte

~ CONTENTS ~

Introduction

Goin' walk and never get tired
I'm goin' move up a little higher. . . .

I met Mahalia Jackson through this song. I heard her sing "Move On Up a Little Higher" on a cassette, and I flipped. I listened to her build the song, phrase by phrase, her rock-steady rhythm growing harder and harder—"'I'm goin' DRINK from the CHRIS-tian FOUN-tain'"—until it became impossible not to tap or snap or clap something. Until it became impossible not to *move*.

I loved the voice. I loved the spirit behind the voice, too. I quickly came to love gospel music, by other singers as well as Mahalia. Here was hymn singing, which I'd always liked, with a beat. Gospel rocked; it let loose. It let *me* loose.

Mahalia's singing freed me to write a different sort of biography. I wanted the story to have music in it; that is, to make the writing musical. Rather than tell everything that Mahalia did, as the writer of a straight biography would, I selected events and experiences that seemed to make her what she was. A young reader, I thought, would want to know such things. How does a person find her way? How does someone get to be great?

My intention was to write a book that would read like a story but was true. All the quotes are real (that is, from published sources), and all the events really happened (again, according to published sources). Even the feelings expressed in the text are verifiable.

Researching Mahalia Jackson's life presented several interesting problems. Was she born, as she and her aunts believed, on October 26, 1912? Or was she born on October 26, 1911, the date on her birth certificate? The 1912 date is the one carved into her gravestone, but most reference books list 1911. After careful thought, I decided to use the official year, 1911, but I believe that Mahalia had the right date and that somebody made a mistake somewhere along the way with her birth certificate.

A more general problem was the task of gathering accurate information about a person who was not in the habit of keeping a diary or of writing letters. Mahalia Jackson "wrote" an autobiography with Evan McLeod White, but it is incomplete and clearly not her voice, but Mr. White's. I relied on the only complete biography, Laurraine Goreau's *Just Mahalia, Baby*, for much of my information. Ms. Goreau lived in New Orleans and knew Mahalia, and her long, conversational book was invaluable. Jules Schwerin's film documentary *Got to Tell It: Mahalia Jackson, Queen of Gospel* and his companion biography of the same name also provided insight.

One source was a thrill to discover. During her early days in Chicago, Mahalia sang from a little brown Baptist hymnal called *Gospel Pearls*. In the New York Public Library I found a worn copy—not her copy, but I felt a connection to Mahalia as I turned the brittle pages.

I felt the connection, too, when I went to my church and sang in the choir, and when I visited New Hope Baptist Church in Newark, New Jersey, which has a strong gospel choir, and Pilgrim Baptist in Chicago, where Mahalia sang. Faith was the essence of Mahalia's being. Praying, singing, and going to church were the most important things in her life, the trinity of her existence. I couldn't have understood that if I hadn't gone to church.

A note on terminology: In Mahalia's lifetime people used the terms *Negro* and *colored* when they referred to African Americans. In the 1960s the word *Black* replaced *Negro*. Since I doubt that Mahalia changed her speech habits much in her late years, and because I wanted to be consistent, I used *Negro* and *colored* throughout the book.

I had been to Mahalia's birthplace of New Orleans while researching a book about Louis Armstrong, but for this book I wanted to explore Chicago, Mahalia's second city. Six hundred thousand African Americans migrated from the South to the North in the early twentieth century. In Chicago they settled on the South Side in a bustling neighborhood called Bronzeville. Urban renewal has destroyed many of the old buildings, including Mahalia's Beauty Salon, which was replaced by the Illinois College of Optometry. Happily, three of Mahalia's homes have survived, and her pretty house on South Indiana Avenue has a marker out front.

On Martin Luther King Drive and Twenty-sixth Place stands a fifteen-foot-high modern sculpture, cast in bronze, of a man carrying a cardboard suitcase bound with rope. He wears a suit made of shoe soles, many with holes in them. The sculpture symbolizes the fifty thousand African Americans who came to Chicago during the Great Migration. Mahalia was one of them, pounding the pavement in search of the promises in the Promised Land.

> *Soon as my feet strike Zion*
> *Gonna lay down my heavy burden*
> *I'm gonna put on my robe in glory*
> *I'm goin' home one day, tell my story . . .*

Here is Mahalia's story.

New Orleans

1911—1927

Born Poor

Halie's legs were crooked from the start. Her mother took her to the doctor soon after she was born, in 1911, and came home with bad news. "He say they got to operate. Break her bones," she said. Aunt Bell wouldn't hear of it. Every night and morning she massaged the little legs, hip to toe, with grease from the dishwater. But still the limbs curved so badly that her feet crisscrossed when she learned to walk.

Halie didn't mind—too much. On little fishhook legs she danced for the white lady her mother and Aunt Bell worked for. While they cleaned the white family's house and cooked the family's meals, Halie entertained. Dance for the sheer delight of it. Sing: "Now, first you put your two knees close up tight, then you sway it to the left, then you sway it to the right." Halie had picked up that song as it drifted out of a barroom in her neighborhood. "Step around the floor kind of nice and light, then you twist around and twist around with all of your

The house where Mahalia Jackson was raised, on Pitt Street, New Orleans.

might." Wild applause from other children was a welcome sound to homely little Halie.

She lived with her mother, Charity; her brother, Roosevelt (called Peter); six aunts; and four cousins—thirteen people crammed into three rooms and a kitchen. The house was so close to the train tracks it shook when a train roared by. Halie's father, Johnny Jackson, lived around the corner, but he wasn't married to her mother, and he had little to do with Halie.

With her aunts all working, she was free to wander her city of New Orleans. Dart to the wharf to watch the men carrying bananas off the steamships. Stop in Audubon Park to roast acorns with cousin Celie and cousin Jack. Stroll up busy Magazine Street and listen to a band on a flatbed truck, playing hot jazz music to advertise a "fish fry tonight." Got two cents? Buy a snowball, shaved ice with sticky syrup poured over top—*mmmm*.

In New Orleans anybody who moved, sang. The man selling charcoal, the woman selling strawberries. "Waaaa-tuh-melon, red to the rime!" "Raaabit, lady! Come on with your pan!" The shoeshine boy sang as he snapped his cloth across a shoe. Children running to the store for their mamas chanted, "Quartee beans, quartee rice, lagniappe salt meat, make it taste nice."

Soon Halie was singing in church, too, the youngest member of the children's choir. She hoped God would notice her and straighten her crooked legs. How could He not notice the scrawny four-year-old with a voice twice as big as she was?

When she was six, something terrible happened. Her mother died suddenly, for reasons nobody could name. Halie and Peter and the aunts made the long journey by train, mule wagon, ferryboat, and

Audubon Park, New Orleans,
where Mahalia roasted acorns
with her cousins.

wagon to the old cotton plantation, west of New Orleans on the Atchafalaya River, where Charity had lived as a girl. They buried her in a plain pine coffin, beside the church, right on plantation ground, where her father, Halie's grandfather Paul, preached. When they got home, discussion of what to do with Halie and Peter was brief. Aunt Duke, whose real name was Mahala, said, "I'm keeping them," and that was that. Aunt Duke was boss, and Halie was named after her: Halie's real name was Mahala, too.

Life with Aunt Duke

The first thing Aunt Duke said was: "No more running in the streets. You going to learn how to work." Peter, who was eight, escaped before the sun was up, scouring the city for odd jobs. Halie, who was six, stayed in the little house Aunt Duke shared with quiet Uncle Emanuel and worked, alone.

Empty the ashes from the cookstove and make it spotless. Sweep the floors. Pound a brick to dust, and use the dust to scrub the floors, a patch at a time, until the cypress wood is creamy yellow.

When Aunt Duke got home, she passed her white handkerchief over everything. If the hankie came away dirty, Aunt Duke took out her cat-o'-nine tails, which hurt in nine places. If there was time, Halie ran to Aunt Bell next door. "Whip her next time, sister. Not this time; next time!" cried Aunt Bell, the sweetest person God ever put on this earth. Bell had nursed tiny baby Halie when Charity had to work those long days. Aunt Bell could keep Aunt Duke at bay, but most times there was no time to run. Halie learned not to cry.

As she grew, so did the list of chores. Clean the flatirons with a chunk of red brick. Pass the irons over a cedar branch to make them slip. Heat the irons on the cast-iron stove, then slide them back and forth over the clothes to take the wrinkles out. Halie sang to the slap, glide, slap, glide of the flatiron, "'I'm goin' down the river, goin' down to the river, goin' to take my rockin' chair. . . .'" She tried to sing it the way she had heard Ma Rainey sing it in one of the tent shows. If she closed her eyes, she could see Ma Rainey's necklace of gold coins shimmering in the lantern light. Halie worked her mouth around the sounds until she got them just right.

Here comes the rain! Hurry, put down the pots and pans to catch the streams. When it rained outside, it rained inside. Aunt Duke's roof was full of holes.

School was only sometimes. When the ironing piled up, Halie stayed home. When one of the aunts was sick, she went to work in her place. When Halie did make it to school, the other children made fun of her too-big hand-me-down shoes, and she burned with shame. Solution: go barefoot. Then winter blew in and turned the sidewalks slippery with ice. What could she do but go ask Daddy for shoes? Visit him in the barbershop he set up in his front room on Saturdays. Climb onto his lap and listen to him coo, "My chocolate drop." Then ask: "Please, Daddy, I need a pair of tennis. I got no money."

"Chocolate, I don't have it." He had four other children by another wife now, and his roof leaked, too.

Everybody's roof leaked in Pinching Town.

Aunt Bell's Prediction

Cousin Fred, Aunt Duke's handsome son, announced he was moving to Kansas City and leaving his babies, Isabell and Brisko, behind. Aunt Duke pulled Halie out of school to mind the babies. She was in the middle of fourth grade. She wasn't alone; in New Orleans plenty of children quit school to tend family. Halie saw them everywhere, carrying bundles of freshly ironed clothes on their heads to help their mamas who worked as laundresses. But having company didn't ease the disappointment any. For her, school had been a chance to learn *and* to escape Aunt Duke's chores.

Scrub the porch. Make those pots and pans shine. Keep the babies out of trouble.

One day Halie, at wit's end, hauled out the Victrola Fred had left behind. Aunt Duke didn't allow his records to be played in her house because they weren't church music. But Aunt Duke wasn't home. Halie turned the crank. Out came Bessie Smith's voice singing, "'Careless love, oh, careless love.'" Halie sang along. Isabell and Brisko sat entranced, quiet at last.

Outside people gathered to listen. "You can't tell one from the other!" they said.

Neighbors weren't the only ones to notice something special about Halie. Aunt Bell stopped beside the porch one afternoon when Halie was shelling peas. She took a long look at the hardworking nine-year-old and said quietly, "Halie, don't you worry. You going to be famous in this world and walk with kings and queens."

"You think so, Aunt Bell?" Halie asked, grabbing Brisko as he was about to fall.

"That's right, baby. I seen it." Aunt Bell was always "seeing" things. She had what they call second sight. Her daughter, Halie's cousin Celie, always said, "Mama, your words are as gold apples in a silver pitcher."

A girl picking beets in 1914. Children, including Mahalia, often had to work instead of going to school.

Aunt Bell's seeing was something to pay attention to, but Halie famous? How? Flinging peas—*ping, ping*—into a bowl, Halie felt tears sting the backs of her eyes. She wanted to believe but could not believe.

As she headed to the train yard to get coal, she felt different with Aunt Bell's words rolling around in her head. Just how did a person become famous, she wondered. They went somewhere and did something important. Fred had gone to Kansas City. Lots of people were going to Chicago. There was enough work in Chicago for everyone. Aunt Hannah had gone to Chicago. Daddy, too, but he came right back. He said the city was too big and full of gangsters. Aunt Hannah stayed; she wasn't afraid of anything.

A horn blew, startling Halie from her dreaming. The train was just rounding the curve. She grabbed hold of the coal car, hooked herself onto it, and kicked off pieces of coal with her bare foot. Isabell darted after the coal pieces and gathered them in a basket to take home for the cookstove. Brisko was busy showing off his elephant dance for the trainman, who gave him a nickel and tossed out two more for Halie and Isabell.

Halie put her nickel in the pocket of her dress and smiled. She would need every penny if she was going to walk with kings and queens.

Church Tonight!

"Halie, want to come in for a slice of butter cake?" a neighbor called from the doorway as Halie hurried by.

"No thank you, ma'am. Church tonight!"

Church was Wednesday and Friday nights and four times Sunday, and Halie never missed. Church didn't mind if you were barefoot. Church took you in when your heart ached from knowing your mother was far away in Heaven. Church was home.

"Let it out, Mahala," shouted Oozie Robinson, the choir director at Mount Moriah Baptist Church. He had a withered arm that jumped when he was excited, and he *was* excited. "'What a friend we have in Jesus, all our sins and griefs to bear,'" Halie sang in her astonishing voice. She was twelve and her voice could be heard to the end of Millerton Street, where it competed nicely with Kid Ory's band playing hot jazz music from a wagon parked on the corner. "'In his arms he'll take and shield thee. Thou wilt find a solace there.'"

*Mt. Moriah Baptist Church,
where Mahalia first sang.*

A solace, yes. What a comfort.

Listen to the preacher preach in a cry, in a moan. Hear him shout in a chant way, a groaning sound. Sing a jubilee, and you don't feel so far from God. The foot tapping and hand clapping all around gave Halie the bounce!

On Sundays Halie arrived at church before sunup, hoping. Yes! The deacon *would* let her ring the bell and press on the electric lights.

First there was prayer service, then Sunday school, followed by the long service at eleven o'clock. Sometimes her grandfather, the Reverend Paul Clark, took the pulpit. Tall, gray-eyed Grandfather Paul still lived on the old plantation and ran the cotton gin in the very place he had been born a slave, but he often came to visit his daughters in New Orleans. He was a licensed Baptist minister, very respected, always had a flock of young ministers-to-be trailing him. His favorite text was: "Seek the Lord where He may be found, and serve Him in your youth." Halie was only too happy to serve.

The choir's slow hymns were good for raising the spirit. "'O God, our help in ages past . . . our shelter from the stormy blast.'" The members of the congregation responded with cries of "Amen" and "Yes, Lord!" Like it says in Psalm 100: "Make a joyful noise unto the Lord. Serve the Lord with gladness: come before his presence with singing." Oh, yes. But it was the jubilees that got the people on their feet, swaying and clapping their hands. When the joy on the inside welled up so strong you couldn't keep still—you had to move. Get happy! The jubilees made Halie feel so *good.*

Between youth group and the evening service came baseball—if you dared. Ball playing on the Sabbath was strictly forbidden in Halie's family. Halie dared. She was shortstop, and she was good. When her punishment came from Aunt Duke, she took the lick of the cat-o'-nine-tails in stride.

The whole family gathered at Aunt Duke's house for Sunday dinner. Feeding people, Aunt Duke became a different person. She laughed. She joked. "I'm Mrs. Paul and I'm on the ball!" Her table groaned under the weight of bowls of sliced tomatoes, potato salad, mustard greens, roast pork with yams and gravy, green beans with pig tails, corn bread, biscuits, and figs and oranges from the trees out back. Everyone in Pinching Town knew Mahala Paul could cook— even beggars knocking at the back door. Aunt Duke never turned anyone away.

Halie ate until she could eat no more, and then she had a slice of butter cake and a tiny cup of chicory coffee strong enough to kill Goliath.

Slip outside. The Sanctified Church was holding its service next door. A beat, a powerful beat, a rhythm from slavery days came up through the porch floor and tickled the soles of Halie's feet. Bang that drum! Shake that tambourine! Through the doors opened wide to catch the river breeze, Halie could see the Sanctifieds singing with their whole bodies. Such a wild holy dance was not to be seen at Mount Moriah. No instruments were allowed. If you wanted a beat, you clapped your hands, at Mount Moriah. Halie stood transfixed.

Aunt Duke called. Clear the table. Heat the water. Scrub the pots.

Halie went back to work, humming with her whole body.

Answered Prayers

Halie's prayers were answered. As she grew, her legs straightened. People said it was a miracle. Maybe. More likely, it was the work of Dr. Jesus, as Grandfather Paul liked to say whenever anyone got over a sickness.

"I am a living witness to the power of prayer," she whispered to the mirror.

Prayer led her to something else, too: baptism. At Mount Moriah, you had to pray to seek the Lord. Only when you found Him were you considered ready to be baptized, and then you still needed the consent of a parent; in this case, Aunt Duke.

Halie was fifteen when she prayed and saw Jesus. Aunt Duke came home to find her niece looking radiant.

"The Lord touched me, Aunt Duke. I have been reborn," she said.

"We'll see." Aunt Duke was not convinced. She had known plenty who said they had *seen* when all they'd *seen* was their own imaginations.

Mahalia was baptized by being submerged in water, like this girl in Louisiana in the 1930s.

In a Friday night service, Halie testified. Standing in the choir loft, she told of her vision of Jesus, and then she sang an old hymn, drawing out the tune, packing all her grief and determination into every word. "'Jesus, my God, I know his name, I wonder where is He....'" She set the church on fire. Aunt Bell, in particular, got so high in the spirit—rocking and twitching, with arms flailing—that she had to be held down by several pairs of hands.

Still Aunt Duke resisted. It took a special visit by a group of church women to persuade her that her niece was ready to be baptized.

The day came, and Mahala Jackson, tall, skinny, and as straight as a bald-cypress tree, walked into the Mississippi River, wearing a long white cotton batiste gown. The pastor, his black robes billowing, plunged her into the cool water, and Halie emerged, clapping her hands for joy.

The next day she felt the world had changed. She told Celie, "I have a desire to serve the Lord in spirit and in truth."

"You always had *that*," Celie said.

"He told me to open my mouth in his name." Halie had received her calling. Whatever else she might do in her life, she knew her true work was to "sing unto the Lord a new song," like it said in the Bible, Psalm 98. "For He hath done marvelous things." Yes, indeed. Amen.

Having a converted Halie in the house made no difference to Aunt Duke. She was the same as ever, wielding the broom handle whenever she was displeased, and making rules. No parties. Be home by 8:30. "Don't let the dark catch you out, you hear me? Unless it's church, and straight back!" Aunt Duke said.

Halie broke the rule early one evening, stopping with Cousin Celie at a party of a married friend. The house was full of people, who spilled out into the yard. Halie, busy with her friends, didn't see a young man start to bother her pretty cousin. When Halie saw Celie struggling in a dark corner of the yard, she grabbed the first thing she saw, an ice pick, and stabbed the man. He wasn't hurt bad.

"Get on home before you catch it," their friends said. The girls flew home, knowing what time it was: 8:30. Aunt Duke beat Halie and then threw her out. Teach her a lesson, she would.

Halie poured out her heart to Aunt Bessie, who was more like a cousin, being just twelve years older. "All right, baby, if you gone, you gone," said Aunt Bessie. Having no one else to take her in, Halie found a tiny house a block from Bessie's, just one room and a kitchen, for six dollars a month. Aunt Bessie brought over an iron bed and a mattress. People in the church gave what they could spare. Everyone grieved for Halie, too young to be living alone in rough-and-tumble Pinching Town, but no one dared cross Aunt Duke. It was like coming up against a stone.

Halie was too busy looking for work to worry about being alone. She cleaned houses for $1.50, sometimes just $1.00, a day, but it wasn't enough. She found a night job, caring for a lady's house and her little girl while the lady worked.

Aunt Duke did not ask her back.

Then Aunt Hannah came home on a week's visit from Chicago— tall Aunt Hannah who was full of stories. She wanted to take neat, prim Celie back with her. Aunt Bell said no.

"Why don't you take Halie?" said Aunt Bessie, whose heart was sore for the girl.

Cousin Baby Williams, who was taller than Hannah, could make her listen. "Charity's in Heaven, resting. You do for her child what she can't do for herself. You take her away, up to Chicago."

On the last evening of her visit, in December 1927, Aunt Hannah was standing on the corner when Halie came along. "Do you want to come to Chicago with me?" she asked.

"Yes!"

"Well, get yourself packed and let's make us a lunch, girl."

On the Illinois Central

"Shove these things up on that rack, Halie," said Aunt Hannah, handing over two suitcases bound with rope. "And keep that lunch where we can get at it, baby."

Halie set the basket full of sandwiches, fruit, and pie, plus containers of water and milk, between them. The dining car was WHITES ONLY, so you had to bring your own lunch when you rode the Illinois Central.

Chicago! Aunt Alice and Aunt Bessie's little Alice were already there. Now she, Halie, sixteen years old, was bound for the Promised Land. She had left in such a hurry, there had been no time to say goodbye to Oozie and the choir, or her other friends. Standing on the porch in the dark early morning, Aunt Duke had cried, actually cried, tears as big as the raindrops pouring from the sky. Celie had howled. Poor Celie, left behind.

Wheeeeee! screamed the whistle. *Sssssbbbb!* hissed the steam. The train moved slowly out of the station.

"No use to cry, 'cause I'm going, I'm really going," Halie whispered.

The green upholstered seat was prickly against her bare legs. There was no heat in the car, and they'd be traveling all today, tonight, and all tomorrow. How thrilling. How scary. Her hand flew to her chest. It was still there, the wad of hard-earned money pinned to her bra. One hundred dollars.

Night fell, and Aunt Hannah pulled a blanket over the two of them. Halie was too restless to sleep.

"Aunt Hannah?" she said softly.

"What, girl?" She was awake, too.

"You think I—you think I could be a nurse?"

"You be anything, you work hard enough. This is Chicago."

Although Mahalia traveled North by train, other African Americans leaving the South went by car, and even by foot—by any possible means.

Chicago

1927—1948

Promised Land

Whoo! The wind! Halie's coat felt about as thick as a potato sack. What was that stinky smell? The stockyards, Aunt Hannah said, where they kill pigs and turn them into pork chops. *Phew!*

From the Twelfth Street Station they took a taxi to the South Side. The driver was white. Halie was astonished. Back home it was against the law for a Negro to ride in a white man's taxi. Not in Chicago. "They're glad to take us," Aunt Hannah explained.

The city lights went on and on as far as Halie could see. And the buildings were so tall. Did people really live in them?

The taxi stopped at a side-by-side double house of gray stone, just three stories high. Could this fine-looking house be home? Yes, 3250 South Prairie was divided into apartments, and Aunt Hannah shared one with Aunt Alice, Little Alice, and a stranger in the room that Aunt Hannah rented out.

Halie got the sofa—and did not get up for a week.

She was overcome with fear. Chicago was so big. All stone and brick and concrete. And so cold. Everyone talked funny, not like New Orleans at all. Nobody would understand her when she opened her mouth in school. School! How could she bear to be in fourth grade again? She was sixteen and five-feet-seven-and-a-half-inches tall!

Sunday came, and Aunt Hannah had had enough. "Come on, get up out of there and let's go to church, and you'll feel better."

They went to a big brick church packed with people. Halie got so filled up with feeling that she stood up in the middle of the service and delivered a solo song, unasked for. "'Hand me down my silver trumpet, Gabriel; hand me down my silver trumpet, Lord,'" she sang in her big voice. To her surprise, she saw frowns among the congregation. It seemed that singing out of turn was not done at Greater Salem Baptist Church. These people had all come up from the South, just like her, but they had thrown off their down-home ways the moment they stepped off the Illinois Central and got a whiff of Smoky Town! Now they wanted to sit quietly in the pews and listen to the choir sing stately hymns—like the white folks did in their churches.

Well, at least the pastor welcomed her; the choir director, too. But he said her voice was too strong for the choir. She would sing the solos—the planned solos, that is. No more spontaneous interruptions. That was fine with Halie, just as long as she could sing. "Hand it down, throw it down, any way you get it down. Hand me down my silver trumpet, Lord."

A family on its way to church in Chicago in 1941.

23

Halie now had the courage—just a shred of it, but enough—to get her feet to take her to school. But no sooner had she started the fourth grade again than she had to stop. Hannah took sick, and Halie went to work, cleaning and cooking, in her place. It was just like old times in New Orleans, only here it hurt more. She had begun to dream a little, just for herself. Instead she had to rise long before the sun. Catch the streetcar in the dark. Take the elevated train uptown. Then hop on a bus and ride, ride, ride. The white family lived far away on the North Side. Cook and scrub until nightfall. Then ride again—bus, el, streetcar—all the way back to 3250 South Prairie.

Hannah got well and returned to work, but for Halie there was no returning to school. The white family wanted her to stay on and wash clothes while Hannah did the cooking and housework. Halie said yes, and in time she found work closer to home, housecleaning for a dollar a day, plus bus fare. The money was welcome at Aunt Hannah's, even needed; Chicago was so expensive. Food especially. Nobody had gardens the way they did back home, so you had to buy your fruits and vegetables. As for meat, mostly you had to settle for State Street chicken, otherwise known as neck bones.

Celie wrote almost every day: Please come home.

Halie wrote back and told her the work was much harder here. "You even have to wash windows."

But she did not go home. She was going to walk with kings and queens, remember? Surely the Promised Land would hold some promises for her. But what promises? When?

A Joyful Noise

Halie's favorite spot in the apartment was next to the radio. Even when the room was full of people, she paid no attention to anything but the voice coming out of the box. "You can learn something," she said. Rudy Vallee, singing out "Heigh-ho, everybody," played all kinds of music on *The Fleischmann Yeast Hour*. Amos and Andy made you laugh every night at seven o'clock. Even the ads were interesting. "Rinso white! Rinso bright! Happy little washday song!" Listening, Halie tried to learn how to leave off that New Orleans back-street brogue and talk like a society Negro. She had discovered that her diction made it hard for people to understand her when she sang.

She was in a quartet now. The Johnson brothers, Robert and Wilbur, and a girl, Louise Lemon, from church, had invited her to join their singing group a few months after she got to Chicago. Aunt Hannah said they could practice in the apartment. Halie glowed from the pleasure of having guests, her first.

The Johnson Singers were one of the first gospel groups to make regular appearances in Chicago. They took their music to church socials and services, and wherever they went—big fancy churches or dim and dusty storefront churches where people sat on folding chairs—they filled the room. "'Looking for the stone that was hewed out the mountain. Looking for the stone that came a rolling through Babylon,'" the four voices sang in smooth harmony.

Now and then, when the others couldn't make it, Halie went alone because she didn't want to miss the opportunity. She didn't even own a choir robe; she had to cover her knees with a shawl while she sat near the altar, waiting. When the time came, tall, thin Halie let herself go and sang with her whole heart and body. If only she had a drum and a tambourine, she could make a joyful noise like the Sanctifieds back home. She made do by clapping her hands and patting her feet on the floor.

She wasn't the only one singing God's words with a bounce. Others, such as Sallie Martin and Roberta Martin, were beginning to put the gospel with jazz, too; and Thomas A. Dorsey, Lucie Campbell, Reverend William Herbert Brewster, and Roberta were writing exciting new songs. Some of the ministers, especially in the big churches, didn't like the new gospel music. How could something jazzy give a religious feeling? The music was unholy, they said.

Halie's new friend Missie Wilkerson had another view. "These preachers jealous of you, Mahala, 'cause you just a slip of a girl and the people coming to listen to you," she said.

"That's all right," Halie said. "One sorrow don't make a day; only the Lord make the day."

One time a pastor took her by surprise when he rose and shouted at her to get that twisting and that jazz out of his church!

Mahalia sang in many storefront churches like this one in Bronzeville.

Halie shot back at him: "This is the way we sing down South! I been singing this way all my life in church. If it's undignified, it's what the Bible told me to do!" She read her Bible every day, and she knew as well as he what the book said. Right there in Psalm 47 it said: "Oh, clap your hands, all ye people! Shout unto the Lord with the voice of a trumpet!"

There were plenty who wanted to hear the voice of a trumpet on Sunday morning in the little basement congregations and the rackety-rack storefronts that dotted Bronzeville, as people called the colored neighborhood on the South Side. She packed those places. "Halie's got something they can clap and rock by!" the people said. They liked a little taste of home in combination with the new gospel sound.

In time the ministers at the big churches began to change their minds and invite Miss Mahala Jackson to sing. "'When I wake up in glory by and by,'" she sang, and people just had to clap or shout. No one could sit still when that voice filled the majestic stone buildings with no help from any microphone. Soon the invitations were coming so fast that she sometimes had to choose between busting suds and singing in church. Singing won out every time, even though pay was no more than supper and a few coins. "Give as you may and will for the singer," the preacher always said, but *after* the collection had been taken for the church.

Hannah charged her rent now; how was she to pay it?

Make tickets for her own programs of gospel songs. Cut the tickets out of shirt cardboard, with Missie. Write "10 cents" on them. At night when nobody's looking, use your shoe to tack signs on poles and fences.

But when the day of the program came, Halie said, "Now, Missie, don't turn nobody down if they ain't got that dime."

It was 1931; the Depression was on. People didn't have two nickels to rub together. They had lost their jobs, and they were hungry and worried sick about their children. Listening to the tall, skinny girl who was so fiery and exciting, they found a moment's joy.

She was twenty. It was time to change her name. Slip an *i* into it: Mahalia. "It sounds pretty that way," she told her aunts. In truth it meant more. *Mahala* was Aunt Duke, boss of the seven Clark sisters, in New Orleans. *Mahalia* rode the Illinois Central for two whole days and one long night and pitched her tent in Smoky Town. *Mahalia* was a fish-and-bread singer in Chicago; she sang for her supper, and she sang for the Lord.

If she could only make it something to live on, pack the iron and the scrub brush away forever. If Jesus could make five loaves of bread and two fishes feed thousands of people because he believed, then she could provide for herself, with God's help. If she believed.

"Let there be light for Mahalia," she prayed.

Romantic Interlude: Ike

Mahalia hardly noticed the man who crossed the crowded room at the Greater Salem social to introduce himself, she was having such a good time with her church friends. But when Isaac Hockenhull, known as "Ike," came to call on her at Aunt Hannah's, Mahalia noticed. He was a well-dressed gentleman with a tidy mustache and the prettiest manners she had ever seen. He had a fine way of talking, too. He was educated, a graduate of the Tuskegee Institute *and* two years at Fisk University. A trained chemist, Ike couldn't find a job at present, so he was working at the post office, temporary.

He took her to the movies and to vaudeville shows—she could sit and watch all afternoon. She was crazy about that funny man Stepin Fetchit in the vaudeville show, and all of Charlie Chaplin's movies, and the one with Bing Crosby, *The Big Broadcast*. On payday Ike escorted her to the Sunset Café to hear Louis Armstrong—just up from New Orleans and already making a name for himself—blow hot jazz on his cornet. Halie from Pinching Town was being courted and taken to theaters and nightclubs! Oh, Ike was grand.

But not too grand to sit in Hannah's kitchen with a hammer in one hand and a towel in the other, making peppermint pickles. Pound the soft outside of the peppermint sticks, thick as broom handles, to get to the hard red core. Break off sticks the length of a pickle. Dig a hole in each pickle for the candy. Together Ike and Mahalia could empty a jar of peppermint pickles as fast as they could fill it—*yumm!*

Louis Armstrong (seated at piano) with his band, the Hot Five, which included his wife, Lil Hardin, on piano.

Mahalia's Vow

Poppa was coming! Aunt Hannah had sent a train ticket to Grandfather Paul to come for a visit. It was an honor to have him in their midst.

And he was so pleased to hear Mahalia sing in church. She liked to sing out of her little brown *Gospel Pearls* book. "His Eye Is on the Sparrow" was one of her favorites, and she had a special way of swooping down on the word *sparrow* like a bird coming in for a landing. "'I sing because I'm happy; I sing because I'm free, for His eye is on the sparrow, and I know He watches me.'"

In gratitude, Mahalia wanted to take Grandfather to have his picture taken—"I got the money!" she said. It was a hot, hot day. At the photographer's studio, Grandfather Paul had a stroke.

All the way to the hospital in the taxicab, Mahalia prayed. Aunt Hannah lashed out at her: "If you hadn't sent Poppa out into that

Mahalia at the beginning of her career.

terrible heat, this never would have happened. His death is going to be on your shoulders!"

Stunned by stinging words from warm, welcoming Aunt Hannah, Mahalia found an empty room in the hospital and dropped to her knees. She prayed to God for forgiveness. "If You will only let Grandfather live, I will make my life as pure as I can." I must give something to God, as a sacrifice, she thought. But what? Movies and vaudeville shows—she loved those above everything. "If You will make Grandfather well, I will never go to a theater again," she prayed.

Grandfather Paul got well, and Mahalia kept her vow. No more movies with Ike. No more Sunset Café to hear Louis Armstrong. And no singing in a theater, ever, for Halie.

Aunt Hannah, relieved, forgave Mahalia, and even entrusted her with the job of seeing Poppa safely home on the train. It was Mahalia's first visit to New Orleans since coming to Chicago seven years earlier, and she basked in the attention from family and friends at Mount Moriah Church. It was a pleasure, too, to sit on the porch with Cousin Celie on a warm evening, to smell the river and listen to the familiar sounds—laughter from the lawn party close by, hot jazz riding the breeze from the honky-tonks. She thought of Chicago, its cold wind and the hard pavement that chewed holes in the bottoms of her shoes. "It's hard but I'm going to try to make it," she told Celie quietly.

Riding North on the train, Mahalia had two whole days and a long night to think about where she was headed on the gospel road. Seemed like more and more churches were asking her to come alone, without the Johnson Singers. If she was going to sing alone she needed a regular pianist who would do for her, learn her arrangements and know her style. Maybe Estelle Allen . . .

Her mind wandered . . . to money. The new job as a maid at the grand Edgewater Beach Hotel, way uptown on North Sheridan Avenue, was good and steady, twelve dollars a week. And she got two dollars for singing at funerals now; it was an honor just to be asked. She might ask Reverend Childs, one of the big ministers in Bronzeville, if she could make a regular thing of his tent revival meetings; he always took up a collection just for the singer.

Her mind wandered again. Ike. He'd asked her to marry him. He was a churchgoing man, steady, nice to look at. *Hmmm . . .*

Married Woman

When Mahalia was twenty-four, she said yes to Ike, and he moved in with her at Aunt Hannah's. The apartment was crowded now: Hannah had taken in an eight-year-old boy off the streets, John Sellers. John became a part of the family, Hannah's godson, and a protégé of Mahalia's. She taught him to read and then to sing. He shared a room with her and Ike, who was kind to him.

Marriage brought surprises.

One evening Mahalia looked up from her Bible to see Ike studying a racing sheet. Her husband a betting man, a gambler who threw money at horses! She had had no idea.

Next she discovered he had plans for her career. Big plans.

"Why don't you stop this low-down type of singing and learn to sing right?" he said one night in the kitchen.

"I'm doing what the Lord set out for me to do, praise His name with it," Mahalia replied.

"You have a voice like a cello and a head like a rock!" he shouted.

"Be glad I don't have a heart like a stone or I'd pitch you out!" she shot back.

Ike wasn't finished. "You can have a *real* career, on the stage, Mahalia, but you can't do it without proper training."

He was right in one way: she had never studied, couldn't even read music. Her diction was still peculiar, and the cause, she knew now, was not only her leftover New Orleans brogue but her way of stretching out syllables and shaping them to make sounds that pleased her. *She* knew what she was singing about, but others didn't always know.

So Mahalia went to see an opera singer famous in Chicago, a colored woman named Anita Patti Brown. Miss Brown did not see any reason for lessons. "Just go on and sing, because you can sing," she said.

Mahalia's first home in Chicago, 3250 South Prairie Avenue.

That should keep Ike quiet for a while, Mahalia thought.

Back home, Ike was already hatching a new plan. "Your big chance!" he said, waving a piece of paper.

Mahalia read the announcement of auditions for *The Hot Mikado*, a theatrical show with an all-Negro cast, and remembered her vow not to sing in theaters. "This got nothing to do with me," she said.

"Halie, nobody can touch your voice! It's not right for you to throw it away hollering in churches!"

She had never seen her husband so mad. He had been laid off from the post office. Money was scarce. She went to the audition.

She sang "Sometimes I Feel Like a Motherless Child," and she *felt* it. She was chancing her soul for a dollar. To hear the people in the auditorium applaud felt like hot grease popping at her.

When she got home, she found Ike excited. The theater people had already called to the apartment next door, where neighbors kindly took calls for Mahalia and Ike, who had no phone, and said she had the job. She would be earning an astonishing sixty dollars a week. And he, by the way, had found a little work, too, selling insurance.

"Thank you, Jesus. I don't have to go on the stage," she said, and went to the telephone to decline the offer. Ike raged. Mahalia stood firm. She had faced the biggest temptation of her life. She had nearly fallen into the pit, but she had resisted. She had triumphed in her time of trial.

"Mahalie's on the Box!"

She was singing at a funeral when a man handed her his business card and said, "I want to put you on records. You had all those people crying." The card read: "J. Mayo Williams, Artists and Repertoire, Decca Records, Race Record Division."

Mahalia fingered and read and reread the business card all night and the next morning. Finally she gathered her courage and telephoned. How much does it cost to make a record, she wanted to know.

J. Mayo Williams, called "Ink," laughed. "Nothing. Just come on down."

Twenty-five-year-old Mahalia gathered her piano player, Estelle Allen, and four gospel songs. Curious, eager John Sellers tagged along. They went to the biggest building she had ever seen, the American Furniture Mart, ten times the size of anything on Canal Street in New Orleans. Mahalia was quiet as she presented gifts to Ink Williams: a bottle of whiskey and a box of cigars.

He was the musical director. He told her where to stand so the microphone could pick up the sound of both her voice and Estelle's piano and organ. In another room, the engineer turned the knobs and pulled the switches. Mahalia had Estelle play piano on the two fast tunes, "God's Gonna Separate the Wheat from the Tares" and "You Sing On, My Singer." Mahalia wasn't a bit nervous as she hollered, holding nothing back, "'If you never hear me sing no more, aw, meet me on the other shore.'" For the slow numbers, "God Shall Wipe Away All Tears" and "Keep Me Every Day," she put Estelle on organ.

Afterward Mahalia, Estelle, and John went out to celebrate with barbecue at a favorite restaurant close to home, but Mahalia had enough money for only two plates of ribs and one bottle of soda pop, and she put some food aside to take home to Ike. When the waitress said to her, "Oh, Mahalia, you're going to be a great singer!" she replied, "No, I don't think so." She wasn't pleased with her first recording. She thought she could do better.

When the record was released in 1938, buyers were few. Gospel music was still fairly new, and confined mostly to the churches. Only one singer, Rosetta Tharpe, had had a hit gospel record, "Rock Me," on which she sang and picked guitar like a bluesman. Rosetta wasn't exactly God-fearing; she'd even sung with the big jazz bands in the dance halls. Mahalia stuck to church and was consequently little known outside of Chicago—unless you counted back home in Pinching Town.

In New Orleans the taverns put a religious record into their jukeboxes for the first time, because this record wasn't by just anybody but by one of their own. The news traveled like fire: "Mahalie's on the box!"

The whole family crowded into the Bumblebee Bar to listen. Aunt Bell had never been in a tavern before, but she dared to enter, along with Aunt Bessie, Cousin Celie, Cousin Allen, and all the other cousins—everyone except Aunt Duke, who was working. Even Johnny Jackson, Mahalia's father, was there. The sound of "God Shall Wipe Away All Tears" boomed from the jukebox, slow and majestic. Everyone listened closely as Mahalia made each word a meditation: "'When we reach the blessed homeland . . . God shall wipe all tears away.'"

In New Orleans, taverns like these on Bourbon Street played Mahalia's first recording in 1938.

"That's my daughter!" cried Johnny Jackson.

Outside, the song blared from other taverns on other corners. Men were crying, wiping their eyes with handkerchiefs. People ran in the streets, shouting, "My God, what a voice!"

In the days that followed, people knocked on church doors in New Orleans, asking to be baptized. Mahalia's voice had that much power.

Back in Chicago, Ink Williams and Decca Records wanted to harness the power. Point it in another direction. How would she like to record some blues and make a fortune?

The blues was not church music. Blues was Bessie Smith and "Careless Love," and that was all right for *her*. Since the day Mahalia was plunged into the muddy waters of the Mississippi, she had tried to heed her calling, to sing unto the Lord a new song. If she opened her mouth, she did it in His name only. Sorry, Mr. Williams. "This is a gift of God. I would have no right to abuse it. I'm doing what the Lord set out for me to do, praise his name with it!"

Decca Records dropped her.

Where was the light for Mahalia?

A Feeling for Hair and the Lord's Business

The light shone—on a vacant storefront diagonally across from the Pilgrim Baptist Church. Mahalia had an idea. Women all over Bronzeville were fixing hair, and some even had their own shops. She and Ike could live in back. Paint it blue. Scrub it clean. Open up a business: Mahalia's Beauty Salon.

She had always had a feeling for hair. Growing up alongside Aunt Duke complaining and fussing with her scrub that was too short for even the shortest plaits, Mahalia knew her own hair was a miracle, a gift from God. Thick and not nappy but hot-comb smooth. She knew just what to do with it, too: sweep it to the top of her head with a roll and a deep wave in front.

Her plan surprised everyone: Ike, Aunt Hannah, Aunt Alice—all except John Sellers. "Told you she could hang on to a dime," he said. He was right: Mahalia had been laying up a bit of money.

But you needed training if you were going to run a beauty shop. Mahalia went to classes at the school founded by Madam C. J. Walker, who had been a millionaire and the first person to make a business out of teaching Negroes how to take care of their hair, to strengthen it and straighten it. Saturdays Mahalia practiced on the head of Emma Bell, a gospel singer and a friend. Styled her hair so many different ways, until Emma couldn't sit in the chair another minute.

When Mahalia's Beauty Salon opened in 1939, customers came at all hours, knowing Mahalia lived behind the shop. They'd even be there before light of day, but she got up; she needed the business.

Madam C. J. Walker.

And business was good. Mahalia received $1.50 a head, $2.00 if there were curls. And she got something she didn't expect: community.

Gospel music was finally taking hold in Chicago, and Mahalia found herself in the middle of a close-knit fellowship of singers. The big churches had come around at last and were clamoring for gospel music in their services, so choirs were being organized. Small singing groups were springing up all over the South Side: the Roberta Martin Singers, led by Roberta, who played piano and wrote songs, and the Sallie Martin Singers, a female quartet, were the busiest. Solo singers were still few. Besides Mahalia, there were Roberta and the hard-traveling Willie Mae Ford Smith from St. Louis, who passed through Chicago often.

All the gospel folks knew to head over to Mahalia's Beauty Salon if they wanted their hair fixed—or their bellies filled. Mahalia could do more on the little "two-eyes" stove in back than most could do in a real kitchen. She cooked down-home Louisiana food: okra with salt pork, red beans and rice, mustard greens. Hot-water corn bread: just water, corn meal, and a little grease; fry it up and eat it. And chitlins—nothing but hog guts, but when they're cooked right, they can be the sweetest part of the hog. One way Mahalia was like Aunt Duke: she enjoyed feeding people.

Weekdays were busy in the shop, but for weekends she hired extra operators so she could be off about the Lord's business. More and more, that meant traveling outside of Chicago. Professor Thomas A. Dorsey had chosen Mahalia out of all the singers in Chicago to be his traveling partner. He was a composer of gospel songs, mostly with a jump-happy beat. He had heard her sing at his church, the grand, gray-stone Pilgrim Baptist, with Stars of David in the stained-glass windows because it used to be a synagogue before the Negroes took

Pilgrim Baptist Church, where Thomas A. Dorsey first heard Mahalia sing, on Easter Sunday, 1941.

it over. Professor Dorsey needed someone to demonstrate his songs, and Mahalia needed good songs to sing on her church programs. They became a team.

"'Precious Lord, take my hand, lead me on, let me stand,'" she sang, breathing heavily and in all the wrong places despite Professor Dorsey's efforts to correct her, decorating the words with extra notes, even changing words, because she *would* make a song her own. He had written the song "Take My Hand, Precious Lord" in response to a tragedy: his wife died in childbirth, and the baby died a few days later. It was a slow, heavy song, born of intense suffering coupled with faith in a helping God, and Mahalia knew something about *that*. "'When my life'"—breathe—"'is al-'"—breathe—"'most *gone*,'" she sang, stretching out the word *gone* and putting a little wave in it. "'Take my hand precious Lo-o-o-o-rd and lee-ee-ee-ead me ho-ho-o-me.'"

Sheet music for a gospel song by Roberta Martin, who also led her own singing groups.

Afterward Dorsey sold the sheet music to the songs she had sung, for ten cents a copy.

Her pay was whatever people offered at the door.

More than once there was nothing at the door for Mahalia, or so the minister said. More than once the preacher threw them out because he didn't like gospel music, saying, "You can't *sing* no gospel; you can only *preach* the gospel," and they spent the night sitting on their luggage in a railroad station somewhere, waiting for the next train. More than once Mahalia and Professor Dorsey were refused a cup of coffee in the station, even though they had the money, because they were Negroes. Sometimes the trains were crowded and grimy, and the air smelled of urine.

Mahalia rehearsing with Thomas A. Dorsey in 1940.

Professor Dorsey was a great man, but traveling with him was wearying, and it peeved her that he made more than she from their trips. "I'm supposed to be a fish-and-bread singer, but all I'm getting is chips," she said to Ike and John when she got home.

Ike was still gambling. Losing mostly, but one time after a big win he bought her a shining, new white Buick. Another time he asked Mahalia to hide a roll of money while she went to Detroit with Dorsey, so Ike wouldn't be tempted to throw it away on the horse races. She flattened out the roll, hid it under a rug, and returned home to find the money gone. Ike had bought a horse.

Mahalia was furious. "You with all your education! It's not enough to lose your money on horses; you got to feed one, too!"

When the bank repossessed the Buick because Ike had not made the payments, Mahalia decided she had had enough. Quietly she put an end to their six-year marriage and got a divorce. She was thirty years old.

"Move On Up"

In a windowless room at radio station WENR in Chicago, the DJ, a white man named Studs Terkel, slipped a 78-rpm record from its paper sleeve and placed it on the turntable. He spoke into the microphone: "There's a woman on the South Side with a golden voice. If she were singing the blues, she'd be another Bessie Smith. What she sings is called gospel. Listen." He set the needle in the groove and the record began to turn. The voice sang, "'I'm going to tell God all about it one of these days. . . .'" Mr. Terkel leaned back in his chair. "Incredible," he said.

There it was, a new beat—a bounce. And that sound! A soaring, healing sound that was hers alone. Mahalia had gone into the recording studio again when she was thirty-five, this time for a small, adventurous company, Apollo Records.

Mr. Terkel played that first Apollo record over and over, and the next one, "I Want to Rest," with its flip side, "He Knows My Heart,"

Studs Terkel, the DJ who championed Mahalia's recordings in Chicago.

but few people were going out and buying the records.

Just when the president of Apollo was about ready to tear up Mahalia's contract, the director of Artists and Repertoire urged one more try. How about "Move On Up a Little Higher"? He had heard Mahalia singing it while warming up one day. It was a long song by the Reverend Brewster about going up to heaven: "'One of these mornings . . . I'm going to lay down my cross and get me a crown. . . . and move on up a little higher.'" Mahalia had picked up the song from another singer, Queen C. Anderson, one time when they shared a program.

She thought through how she wanted to sing it, make it slow, with a steady marching beat. Build and build it, on and on, up and up, "'We gonna LIVE on forever,'" make the beat stronger, *sit* on the beat, "'gonna move on up a little higher, gonna meet my loving mother'"—that line her own addition—until there's nothing a body with ears in his head can do but catch the rhythm and *move*. Do it with piano and organ together, something new. Get James Lee on piano and for organ, James Francis, called "Blind Francis."

They rehearsed all day and into the night. At three o'clock in the morning, they cut the record.

Happy New Year, 1948! "Move On Up a Little Higher" sold fifty thousand copies in Chicago alone in four weeks! Apollo couldn't press enough records to keep up with the demand. Even people who didn't go to church were buying it. They didn't know Mahalia Jackson, but they knew a voice with the power of a Bessie Smith was telling a story they understood: *Moving up.* That's what they had come to Chicago for. And the sound was close to the rhythm-and-blues records they were dancing to.

Mahalia did her part: Deliver the records to the stores. Sell the records at the concerts, going up and down the aisles at intermission. "Don't bother making no change for eighty-nine cents," she told her helper friends. "Sell them for a dollar." The eleven-cent difference she put into her pocket. Like John Sellers said, Mahalia could hold on to a dime.

Mahalia in a publicity shot and an Apollo record label from the 1940s.

John Sellers, known as Brother John, was raised by Mahalia's family, and she taught him to sing.

Radio helped, too. Studs Terkel wasn't the only disc jockey spinning gospel records. Chicago now had stations run by Negroes, which aired gospel and its cousin, rhythm and blues, all day long. "All right, children, here's 'Surely God Is Able.' Better put on your shouting shoes," the gospel DJ would announce in an excited voice. "Surely God Is Able" was a hit record from the Ward Singers from Philadelphia. Other groups had successes, too, like the Swan Silvertones with "Lord I've Tried." But Mahalia's record outplayed them all.

"Move On Up" sold one million copies, making her known not just in Chicago but in other parts of the country. Her fee went up, to as much as fifteen hundred dollars for a concert in a big hall (in churches, she took only what they could afford). She got herself an agent, a white man named Harry Lenetska, who had helped Ella Fitzgerald, the Ink Spots, and other top Negro entertainers. He worked to get bookings in auditoriums and concert halls, taking 10 percent of her earnings for himself.

What did she do with all the money? She couldn't put it in a bank. Mahalia didn't trust banks—for good reason. Bronzeville banks were mostly small, flimsy operations, as likely to close down as to open on any given day. Better to carry large sums in a suitcase or a big pocketbook and rely on relatives or close friends to keep the money safe.

And so there she was, on a visit to John Sellers—grown now, calling himself Brother John and singing the blues in New York City—pulling money from her suitcase, pocketbook, girdle, stockings, and bra and piling it on the bed. Count it, recount it, and count it again, it *still* came to forty thousand dollars. "John, you the only one I trust this with," she said, stowing the money in his dresser drawer.

48

With all the bookings coming in, she was too busy to run the beauty shop, and she sold it. But no sooner had she given up the shop than she started another business: Mahalia's House of Flowers. She had always had a feeling for flowers, growing up alongside Aunt Bell digging among her pots on the side porch. Now people who wanted Mahalia to sing for funerals were told that she would gladly sing—as long as they bought their flowers from her shop. She knew how to earn a dime, too.

On the Road
1948 — 1956

Meeting Mildred

Mahalia needed a piano player. The bookings were rolling in, and although she had more pianists than she could count who were ready to play for her, she couldn't count *on* any one of them.

"I need somebody who can stick, and I mean stick their behind in that seat," she told one of the more regular pianists, Robert Anderson, who was busy with his own singing career. "Somebody who can get my style."

He suggested Mildred Falls. Mahalia knew the name. Mildred was good, but—"Robert, you got to break this girl in. She's got it, but she hasn't got it yet."

Before long Mildred knew all Mahalia's arrangements by heart. Soon it was only Mildred who knew how to follow Mahalia when she sang. Only Mildred could feel the beat exactly as Mahalia did. Mildred could pound out the chords just right to keep a fast song dancing. On a slow song, she rippled and rolled the chords underneath Mahalia's long, sustained notes. Only Mildred knew what to do when Mahalia got in the spirit and stretched a song, adding lines of text here and moans there, responding to the audience that shouted its approval. Mahalia might use other pianists now and then, but meek, mild Mildred, fifteen years younger than Mahalia, "stuck"— for twenty years.

Their first tour of the South together was Mildred's baptism. Mahalia got sick on the train, and Mildred had to take over—Northern-born Mildred, who was ignorant of segregation Southern-style. She helped Mahalia off the train at their final stop, then onto a bus. Careful: Let the white people on first. Go sit in the back with the other Negroes, yes'm. Carry the luggage onto the bus, piece by piece, wondering: Where had all the porters gone? Vanished at the sight of her, that's where—and here's the white bus driver, snarling.

In a South Carolina town, Mildred got off the bus and located a taxi for colored. She loaded Mahalia in, then headed back for the bags

In the 1950s, African Americans in the South were required by law to sit in the back of the bus.

and boxes. Spying two white boys with a baggage cart, she asked in a small voice, "I have quite a bit of luggage on the bus. Would you help me, please?"

"Who you think you are, gal?" one boy growled. Mildred watched as the cart rolled past.

Then the colored taxi driver didn't want her to put the luggage in his cab. He thought she was too uppity, talking to white boys. But when he tried to back up his car to leave, the boulder of bags and boxes blocked his way. Mildred won a small victory when the driver put Mildred, Mahalia, *and* their luggage into the taxi. During the ride Mildred broke down, sobbing, and Mahalia said, "You not a Southern girl."

"No, I'm not," said Mildred.

"I can see you not."

The sulky driver wouldn't take them all the way to the hotel, but left them off a block away, in the pitch dark. Sitting on the bags while Mahalia checked into the hotel, Mildred grew more and more afraid. What if a white man came by? What would he say to her, or do . . . to . . . her? By the time the man arrived to carry the bags, she was in tears again.

She cried through dinner and a bath.

"Mildred—talk," said Mahalia, impatient, tired, still sick.

Mildred talked. And talked. "I never see anything like this! I heard of it, and you know I didn't say anything when it's 'No, we don't have one' when there's a 'clean restroom' sign right in our face; and I've seen them do some things, but this is the first I've experienced of it; this is the worst. My own people wouldn't help me!"

The conversation continued all night long, with Mahalia telling how things went down South and Mildred weeping and railing against things she did not—would not—understand. Being in the South was like being in another country, Mahalia explained. The laws were

Segregated restrooms in the South around 1960.

different down here. Separate everything for white and colored: drinking fountains, waiting rooms in the train and bus stations, restaurants, hotels, schools—everything "separate but equal," but you know it was never *equal*, just better for the whites and worse for the Negroes. You never get a clean bathroom behind a door that says COLORED ONLY.

Another thing: Colored don't speak to white, much less ask for help. And that taxi driver, he wasn't mean; he was just afraid, Mahalia said. Probably had a wife and children, and he didn't want to get lynched for driving two ignorant Negroes from up North who didn't know their place.

Mildred wept. Who could blame her?

Certainly not Mahalia. In the morning she got ice to put on Mildred's puffy eyes. That night, at a Negro college, Mildred played and Mahalia sang, their bond fortified by a shared hurt for which there was no healing.

Conquering Carnegie

Mr. Lenetska called, excited. "Max Gordon wants to sign you for five thousand dollars a week at the Village Vanguard. That's a nightclub and this man is famous in New York. A lot of big people would see you."

Here comes the Devil again, Mahalia thought, throwing temptation in my face. "Thank the man kindly, Mr. Lenetska, but the Devil won't catch me there, singing God's songs in a nightclub pleasure house. *Unh-unh!*"

Now, Carnegie Hall, that was different. It was a concert hall for piano and vocal recitals and symphony concerts in New York City. When a disc-jockey-turned-gospel-promoter, Joe Bostic, asked her to sing in the first Negro Gospel Music Festival he was staging at Carnegie in 1950, she said yes—and then got scared. She, Halie Jackson from New Orleans, delivering the gospel in a place where orchestras and opera singers usually were? Her type of music wasn't *high* enough for Carnegie Hall. *She* wasn't high enough for Carnegie Hall.

Mahalia threw up in the car all the way from Chicago to New York, from nerves. Mildred was so sick, she had to check into a hospital on arrival, but with her the cause was food poisoning.

"Lord, pull her through, and me, too," Mahalia said.

The next day she tried to rehearse with her organist Louise Smothers, who had never played for Mahalia before. Mahalia found she had a voice no bigger than a little bird's. They had to quit the rehearsal after one number.

Concert day, October first. Mahalia awoke at five o'clock and knelt on the floor to pray. She ordered hot tea from room service. Mildred walked in—weak but ready, an answered prayer. "Well, I might have known you wouldn't miss Carnegie Hall," Mahalia said. "Want some hot tea?"

They arrived two hours early for the afternoon performance, to find that every seat had been sold. Mahalia was on last, after the gospel groups: the Ward Singers, from Philadelphia; the Cornerstone Baptist Church Chorus, from Brooklyn, New York; and others. While she waited, a friend who was both a pastor and a tailor dressed her in the black velvet robe, edged in white, that he had made for her. She felt like a priest in it.

Then it was on to business: She sent word to Mr. Bostic that she must have her money before going onstage. She got paid in full before the performance—that was her policy.

It was time to pray. Asking her pastor friend to lead the prayer, she meditated, eyes closed, her palms pressed together, for a long while.

Mr. Bostic came in with her fee in hand. A full house, he reported, at least 20 percent white.

At last it was Mahalia's turn. She walked onstage—a tall, substantial

Carnegie Hall,
New York City,
in 1938.

woman of thirty-eight with queenly bearing and eyes that shone when
she smiled—and made the mistake of thinking about where she was:
"Me, a washwoman, standing where such people as Caruso and Lily
Pons stood." She got cold chills. When she started to sing, accompanied by Mildred on a beautiful nine-foot Steinway piano and Louise
on a new Hammond organ, her voice quivered and quavered, but she
plowed ahead. "'Just as I am without one plea,'" she sang. "'Oh, Lamb
of God, I come, I come!'" The audience began to turn and twist;
people were getting in the spirit. "'It pays to serve Jesus, all the way,'"
Mahalia sang, and began to turn and twist, too. She closed her eyes
and sang; she clapped her hands in inspired places. She held her
slender fingers, prayerlike, in front of her ample chest. She fell to her

knees, singing, lost in the music, borne high by the Holy Spirit. "'Amazing grace, how sweet the sound. . . .'" People screamed; they walked the floor.

Suddenly she realized where she was and straightened up. "We'd best remember we're in Carnegie Hall, and if we cut up too much, they might put us out," she told the audience. The crowd settled down some, and when Mahalia continued, she had no more fear of people or place.

Resting at the Theresa Hotel in Harlem, where all the colored entertainers stayed because the big hotels downtown were for whites only, she listened, eyes dancing, as her manager ticked off the offers that had poured in. Columbia University. TV. Europe. She was going to Europe!

Hit the Road

But first: Michigan. Florida. New York. The Carolinas. Mahalia took the singing dates where they fell, and they fell mighty close together in 1951 and 1952. Mostly she drove, or rather, her cousin Little Allen or her friend Robert Anderson, a busy gospel crooner himself, drove the big black Buick that carried her, Mildred, and organist James Lee.

Traveling in the South was hard, after living up North for so long. Mahalia had grown accustomed to white people treating her with respect, even love, for the most part—all those white folks falling all over themselves with appreciation for her in Carnegie Hall, remember? She couldn't go into a department store down South and get a sandwich and a bottle of pop at the lunch counter because she was colored. And here she's the same Mahalia Jackson getting hugged and kissed to death by white folks up North. It didn't make sense. She might be able to tell it to Mildred, explain the rules, the whys, and the wherefores, but none of it made any real sense.

A big, fancy automobile full of Negroes was not a welcome sight in the South. Gas stations wouldn't sell gas to them. Restaurants near the main highway wouldn't serve them. Even drive-in restaurants were off-limits: the white teenage waitresses—carhops, they called them—came bouncing out to the car, saw it was full of Negroes, and spun around and walked away without a word. Mahalia and her friends learned to keep bags of cold cuts and fruit in the car. That's how Mahalia put on weight, not being able to eat regular, balanced meals. Before she knew it, she was up to two hundred pounds.

Need to use a restroom? Better find a bush. Tired? Sleep in the moving car because all the motels just off the highway are for whites only, and there's no time to go searching up and down the byroads just for a bed. Just make sure the car is the roomy, easy-driving kind, so everybody gets a halfway-good night's sleep.

Hurt and angry, Mahalia managed to keep her eyes on the prize. "Put your mind on the gospel we going to sing tonight. And remember, there's one God for all."

Hit the road. Drive till the sun comes up in—Texas. At a Baptist Church in Corpus Christi, Mahalia noticed to her surprise that the audience was mixed—white and colored. But the races sat apart in two bunches on the main floor, and Negroes filled the balcony.

Flashing her shining smile from the pulpit, she said, "Some of you people in the balcony might want to come on down here in front; got some seats down here. And any of you folks rather sit back a little from the singing, feel free to take any seat that's vacated." Then she stood still and waited. First there was a shuffling of feet, then a shifting of bodies as people got up and changed their seats. With a few quiet words, Mahalia had integrated her first mixed audience in the South.

Hit the road and put your mind on the gospel. On to . . . New York City. Apollo Records gave her a gold-plated stamper signifying she was a "million-seller," meaning that her records, not just "Move On Up" but others made since then, were selling a million copies. She couldn't resist inviting John Sellers to her room at the Theresa Hotel. Lock the door, John. Open that suitcase over there. Take out the underwear, all of it. John stared. There in a neat layer were bundles of thousand-dollar bills, sixty in all.

"Now, that's what you call money," she said.

"Mahalia, you not afraid to carry all that around?" he asked.

"Nobody's going to mess with old underclothes," she said.

Mahalia was nobody's fool, even if she was an unlearned woman who had only made it to the fourth grade. She was wise to all the slick promoters, white and Negro, who tried to get a free ride on the gospel train. In Newark, New Jersey, there was one who tried to put off paying her, saying he had booked her through another promoter. Mahalia told the man: "You can just forget about any deal you made with that crook, and start making some financial arrangements right now with me, and I mean cash on the line." She took a seat in his office and waited. Listen to the people out in the concert hall stamp their feet and make a fuss. Ask: "Now then, do I get paid or do I call me a taxi?" After a lot of scurrying back and forth with the cash box, the man handed Mahalia a roll of bills. She put the roll deep down in her pocketbook and went out and sang for the people.

Hit the road on may-pop tires—what people on the gospel road called their worn, old tires: may pop at any moment! Home to Chicago for a few days of rest and to check up on the flower shop. What's this? A thick envelope for her from Mr. Lenetska, containing more contracts for more one-nighters, including two in the very state she had just come from. What to do but head back out directly, before James even had a chance to get the luggage out of the car—"'cause I got to sing."

Hit the road with your mind on the gospel, but don't forget family. In New Orleans, stop to visit her brother, Peter, married now and breaking his back working the wharves.

"Let me give you a trip to Chicago," said Mahalia.

"We'll see," said Peter. Cousins, other family, and friends: plenty had their hands out now that Mahalia had cash to spare. But not Peter. He was too proud.

Hit the road and watch the gas! No time to stop for lunch. Sorry, Robert. He was driving and complaining about being hungry. They were *all* hungry. Mahalia promised that the sponsor in Harrisburg, Pennsylvania, would have a meal prepared for them. They arrived, stomachs growling, at a lovely house, to find a table laid prettily with tuna salad, cheese dip, punch, and, for Mahalia, hot tea (she always drank tea before a performance). A ladies' tea party. Mahalia's jaw dropped.

"Wait a minute, lady. I got to sing tonight—this is air. Give me some food," she said.

As the woman began making excuses, Mahalia exploded. "Well, I'm not going on nobody's program—not until I eat. These folks here is hungry."

She sat down.

The poor woman fled to the kitchen and managed to produce a full meal before Mahalia left for the auditorium. "We sure ate," said Robert.

Hit the road.

Mahalia and her accompanist, Mildred Falls, in Chicago around 1954.

Europe Cut Short

Mahalia could not believe her ears. Her trusted physician, Dr. William Barclay, was telling her she shouldn't go to Europe. One: she needed a hysterectomy. She had been bleeding lately; that was the womb needing to come out. Two, and this was more serious: she had been fighting for breath, and the trouble was in her lymph glands. Before performances, she gasped, trying to find her breath, but then she was always all right the moment she reached the stage or the altar—thank you, Jesus.

"You'll have a rough trip if you go," said Dr. Barclay.

"Don't you worry 'bout Halie. I got strength in my mind," she said. She hadn't come all the way from Pinching Town to cancel her first trip across the Atlantic Ocean for a little medical trouble. And she planned to go on to the Holy Land after the tour, to spend Christmas where Jesus lived and breathed.

Telling no one of her condition, she got on a plane and arrived, feeling weak but determined, in Paris. "Just tired, baby, but I be all right," she told a flock of newspaper reporters and critics who greeted her at the airport.

But come her first performance, at the Salle Pleyel, she gasped for air and burned with fever backstage. "Harry," she sputtered to her agent, "read me"—breathe—"the Twenty-seventh Psalm."

"'The Lord is my light and my salvation; whom shall I fear?'" he read. "'The Lord is the strength of my life; of whom shall I be afraid?'"

Mahalia sat up. "Mildred, God spoke. He said, 'You are healed.' I believe it! I am healed!"

Still gasping, Mahalia walked onstage. She then breathed easily. She sang the gospel; she got happy and danced. The French people gave her a standing ovation, and they didn't even understand the words she sang! Mahalia's ability to gather up her faith and shower it upon an audience like so many grains of wedding rice was that strong.

Offstage, she collapsed. Perspiring, panting, spent, she didn't know if she could ever go onto a stage again.

The pattern repeated itself the next night. And the next. Through Lyon, Bordeaux, London, Oxford, Birmingham; through Holland and Belgium; through Copenhagen. Ill and feeling unable to perform, Mahalia would pray, go on, and rally, delivering a mighty performance to roaring applause, even tears—and this from mostly white audiences who knew gospel music only from records, if at all. Offstage, she would collapse into whatever or whomever was handy and refuse all visitors.

Mahalia was still determined to finish the tour and get to the Holy Land, but when she stopped in Paris on her way to Rome, the French doctors told her that she must go to the hospital. With a heavy heart, she canceled the rest of the tour. She put her dream of following in Jesus' footsteps on hold and flew home. In Chicago she had the surgery, lost her womb at age forty-one. The problem in her lymph glands was called sarcoidosis, Dr. Barclay said. The disease had no known origin and no cure, but it could be controlled, he assured her, with medication and diet.

Mahalia convalesced at Aunt Hannah's, her refuge. Aunt Alice cooked the lean food that the doctor had ordered, and Missie Wilkerson, Mahalia's friend since the early Chicago days, brought over some greens and hot-water corn bread to help the strange meals go down more easily.

Lying in bed, Mahalia had time to think. She didn't need Harry Lenetska anymore. She could get bookings on her own, for the time being, anyway. What she needed was a secretary, someone to hold it all together—concerts, church programs, recordings, autograph signings, press interviews, and requests to sing on the radio. What about Polly Fletcher? She had been running errands for Mahalia for some time. Make Polly secretary. Better tell Emma Bell to teach Polly how to make her hot-water corn bread, if Polly was going to be hanging around all the time.

The flower shop. She'd have to give it up. Impossible to run, now that she was so busy with the Lord's business. Give the store to the woman who had been doing such a good job managing the place in her absence.

What Mahalia really wanted, she realized, was a weekly radio show all her own. If she gave more of her concerts on radio, she could cut down on the traveling, the one-night hops across state lines, that wore her out.

She got well. "It's good I was sick, 'cause God showed me His strength," she said.

A Radio Show and a Rusty Old Halo

Her radio show, it turned out, was just round the corner. While she was in New York and staying at the Wellington Hotel—her first white hotel, very nice (she was successful enough now to lodge there without raising eyebrows)—Mahalia got an offer from Columbia Records. Columbia was big time. The people who bought Columbia recordings were mostly white. The company didn't know anything about gospel music, but the records would sell millions of copies and make her a lot of money. She prayed on it—"What You think Halie ought to do?"— then signed the contract.

A half-hour radio show with her name on it, out of Chicago, was part of the deal; the company thought a regular radio program would sell records.

And so Mahalia went to the magnificent, white-stone Wrigley Building—with its lacy decorative stonework and triangular shape, it looked like a tall slice of wedding cake—to tape her first radio show before a live audience of four hundred, mostly white, listeners. During the warm-up, she had to teach them how to clap along with her singing: off the beat, not on. And she had to tell the Negroes not to jump up and down and stomp when they got in the spirit. "You got to remember, we're not in church; we're on CBS."

When it came time to roll the tape, she found she wasn't used to watching a clock: twenty-five minutes left, twenty, now ten. But with Mildred sending ripples of melody from the piano and that singing quartet of white boys sounding so sweet and smooth, Mahalia could begin to forget the ticktock. She set two old spirituals rocking, "Joshua Fit the Battle of Jericho" and "Didn't It Rain"—got the audience so riled up, in fact, that the Columbia man had to call an intermission. She calmed the people down with "Summertime" and made a few eyes watery, even wet. The lullaby was an unlikely choice, not being a religious song, but Mahalia put so much feeling into her singing that it became almost a prayer. "'So hush, little baby, don' yo' cry. . . .'" One minute left, then zero. The producer ran from the recording booth. "We've got us a show!" he shouted.

On Sunday evening, September 26, 1954, Mahalia sat in her living room, feeling anxious, thinking that people should be in church—*she* should be in church!—and not sitting by the radio. At 9:30 a white man's voice announced, *"The Mahalia Jackson Show,"* and her doorbell rang. It was Ike, come to listen and keep her company. They sat beside the radio, Mahalia following intently every note and nuance. When the show was over, she said to Ike, "I could've been better."

Critics, though, liked her. The station received so many calls and letters that CBS decided to broadcast Mahalia every Sunday night, by herself and with guest choirs and small groups.

TV was a different story. When Mahalia suggested to CBS-TV that she have a regular program, a kind of variety show with herself as host, all she got was silence. Then somebody explained that the show had to have a sponsor, and sponsors wouldn't take a chance on a Negro show because they were afraid that whites in the South would stop buying their products if the products were shown on a Negro program.

Mahalia couldn't believe her ears. "In the name of the Lord, what kind of people could feel that way?" she asked, but all she got was silence.

It was true. The TV had no Negroes except for Ethel Waters, who played a maid in a sitcom called *Beulah*. Mahalia could appear as a guest on the variety shows of other top entertainers, and in time she did: Dinah Shore's, Steve Allen's, and Ed Sullivan's. And she made short films of one song each for TV stations to use as fillers for their end-of-the-day sign-offs. But she never got her own television program.

Then CBS canceled the radio show after twenty weeks because the company couldn't find a national sponsor.

Angry and disappointed, Mahalia managed to put the whole radio/TV mess behind her and set her mind on her recording work with Columbia. That was her way. But a seed had been planted. It was tiny, like the mustard seed in the Bible: "the smallest of all the seeds, but when it has grown it is the greatest of shrubs and becomes a tree, so that the birds of the air come and make nests in its branches." Her seed was a grain of resentment toward the injustices poured upon her people. Seats in the back of the bus. Snarling white faces behind the wheel. Filthy "colored" restrooms next to clean "whites only" ones. Rundown back-o'-town hotels. TV with no black faces on the screen. Separate restaurants, swimming pools, schools. Separate but *not* equal. Never equal.

Expect a sprout any day now.

* * *

*Mahalia in a Columbia
Records studio in 1958.*

Among the songs on Mahalia's first record with Columbia was an old
hymn: "'My faith looks up to thee, thou lamb of Calvary, savior
divine....'" She was working herself into a mighty fervor when the
producer called, "Cut!"

She stopped, frowning. "Why you always shout 'Cut!' just when
the spirit's on me?" she asked. Columbia Records was paying her hand-
somely, fifty thousand dollars a year for four years, and she had to
record only four times a year, but the company would need to learn
something about gospel music if it was going to get along with its
newest client.

She had brought two new songs by her old friend Thomas A.
Dorsey: "Walk Over God's Heaven," a jump-happy rhythm-and-blues
number, and the gentle, loping "It Don't Cost Very Much." Mitch

Miller, the talent chief who had wooed her to the company, had other ideas. He wanted her first Columbia release to be "A Rusty Old Halo." Mitch was quite a salesman. But a waltz about a rich, mean old man who manages to make it into heaven and then all he gets is a rusty old halo? "Sweetened-water stuff," she called it. Definitely not a gospel song. Gospel songs were more than entertainment. They were deep songs that brought back the communication between you and God.

She recorded "A Rusty Old Halo" for Mitch but was disturbed enough to call Aunt Bessie long distance—a consultation. "He wants my records to be more popular," Mahalia explained.

"God is the most popular person in the world," Aunt Bessie said. "'Popular' is God! And remember, baby, He loves you best."

Bessie was right, of course.

Mitch Miller working with Mahalia in the Columbia studios in 1958.

So was Mitch. "A Rusty Old Halo" became a huge hit on colored *and* white radio stations. *Variety* rated the song a "Best Bet" along with "Ko Ko Mo" by the very popular white singer Perry Como. With the silly-sweet halo song, Mahalia crossed the color line completely. She gained acceptance in the white world and became a star.

But she also recorded, at the same session, Dorsey's foot-stomper "Walk Over God's Heaven" as a duet, a calling-back-and-forth between her and a guitarist. It was a smash, too—on Negro radio. Let Columbia and Mitch worry about the white folks. Mahalia knew what her people wanted to hear.

"A Rusty Old Halo" made her a pile of money. She knew just what to do with it, too. Mahalia was going to buy herself a home.

A Home for Mahalia

It was love at first sight. A solid red-brick ranch house with seven
rooms, a pretty picture window, a garage, and plenty of yard in back
to grow some greens. Come Christmas, there would be room enough
in the front yard for the nativity scene she'd dreamed of. The house
stood on the corner of Eighty-third and Indiana in a grassy, tree-lined
neighborhood on Chicago's South Side.

Mahalia wanted the house. She had the money, and the owner
was willing to sell to her. There was only one problem: the neighborhood was all white. The real estate agent said that the neighbors
would make trouble if she moved in.

Mahalia had worked long and hard for a house. God had taken
her from the swamps of the Mississippi to the streets of Paris, and now
to a home on a quiet Chicago street in 1956. Why shouldn't she have
her dream house?

The mustard seed, planted when she couldn't get her TV show, sent up a sprout. It had been watered by the news coming from down South: That fourteen-year-old Negro boy, Emmett Till, who said, "Bye, baby," to a white lady clerk in a grocery store in Money, Mississippi, and a week later, his body was pulled from the Tallahatchie River. And the seamstress in Montgomery, Alabama, Rosa Parks, who decided she was tired of giving up her bus seat to white folks and set off a citywide boycott. Fifty thousand Negroes had been walking or car-pooling to work for months. The Montgomery bus boycott was the country's first sustained civil rights protest. Well, Mahalia was going to mount a little protest of her own, in Chicago.

"I'm a Negro and they don't want me in that house, but I want that house," she told her new agent from the big-talent William Morris Agency, Lou Mindling.

"All right, but don't think of paying in cash," Mr. Mindling said.

Mahalia paid forty thousand dollars for the house—in cash.

Mahalia's house at 8358 Indiana Avenue, Chicago.

The threatening phone calls started immediately. "Your songs aren't going to help you when we blow up your house," one voice said. Before she could move in, someone fired air-rifle pellets into the picture window, shattering it.

Mahalia called Mayor Richard Daley, who was by now a personal friend, and he sent a police guard. The guard protected the property day and night for several months. The calls continued, but she moved in anyway.

Her first night in the house, she phoned her friend Emma Bell. "Come out here, girl. I can't stand this. I can't hear nothing but crickets." It was after midnight, but Emma got into a taxi and rode down to spend the night—and stayed for two weeks, until Mahalia was used to her new surroundings.

Louis Armstrong, now a world-famous jazzman and a friend, was among her first visitors. "Sugar, how you stand this fresh air?" he joked. He sampled her rice and beans and admired how it looked just like New Orleans inside with all that fancy French furniture, the kind white folks had back home.

On Sunday mornings she sat in the garden, to listen. "It's so quiet, all you hear is the birds singing," she said.

Meanwhile, FOR SALE signs began popping up all around her. One by one the white families moved out of the neighborhood and colored families moved in, until Mahalia no longer had any white neighbors. The grass stayed green. On Sunday mornings it was still quiet.

Fame

1956 — 1967

Singing for the Walking People

The bus boycott started by Rosa Parks in Montgomery, Alabama, was still going on almost a year later. Colored people still walked to their jobs, and whites drove alongside them and threw rotten eggs and vegetables. Someone had thrown a brick at a boy. A boy! Negroes' homes had been bombed, but no one had been killed—yet.

Finally, in November 1956, the United States Supreme Court handed down its decision: Segregation on buses was illegal. No more sitting in the back of the bus. No more giving up a seat to the white man. It was a great victory, but the actual order would take days and maybe weeks to arrive, and in the meantime the boycott must continue. The night of the decision, forty cars of Ku Klux Klansmen in white hoods drove through the Negro neighborhood to scare folks into surrender.

Montgomery was no place to be, but what else could Mahalia say when Reverend Ralph Abernathy, a brave and steady young preacher, a boycott leader who had suffered arrest and jail, called and asked her to take part in an Institute on Nonviolence and Social Change to celebrate the Supreme Court decision and commemorate the first anniversary of Rosa Parks's act?

"Of course I'll come, Reverend. I'll come for whatever service," Mahalia replied.

And her fee? "I don't charge the walking people," she said.

Mahalia wasn't feeling very courageous as the train pulled into Montgomery, and she was glad when Reverend Abernathy and another, younger preacher, the Reverend Martin Luther King Jr., were there to meet her and Mildred at the station. Mrs. Abernathy gave up her bedroom to Mahalia and Mildred, and cooked up a tasty mess of greens, and corn bread and ham hocks. All night long, hecklers drove slowly past the house, shouting threats and honking their horns.

At breakfast the Reverend casually mentioned that the church across the street had been bombed not too long ago. Mildred stifled a groan. Mahalia put on a brave face, for Mildred. But after breakfast she slipped away to stand in a nearby cornfield, to pray. "Lord, let Halie make it here, and I'll stand like another stalk."

Her performance wasn't until later in the week; in the meantime she went to the lectures. The Civil Rights movement was unfolding before her very eyes! Reverend King was the best speaker by far, and he was only twenty-seven years old. We are living in "one of the most momentous periods of human history," he said in a slow, clear voice that beamed intelligence. The old order of white supremacy was dying out, and a new order of community was fast approaching, he said. But Negroes must first unite in a mass movement based on non-violence. "This dynamic unity, this amazing self-respect, this willing-ness to suffer, and this refusal to hit back will soon cause the oppressor to be ashamed of his own methods." A new day was coming, he said, when people in America would live together in Christian brother-hood, and "when this day finally comes, 'The morning stars will sing together and the sons of God will shout for joy.'" In all her church-going Mahalia had never heard such a preacher.

Mahalia's turn to testify came on December 6. The big church was packed by noon, and the concert not till eight o'clock! Loudspeakers set up outside would carry the program to those who couldn't fit into the church.

What to sing? What songs would capture the many moods adrift in a troubled city, victorious but weary, afraid and fearless, angry and proud? With her eyes shut, Mahalia opened with a soft, slow number, "A City Called Heaven." She drew out the syllables and twisted them, so that it was hard to make out the words—"'I'm striving to make heaven my ho-oh-u-uhm'" (home)—but the feeling was clear; this was a sorrow song. It brought to mind all the uncertainties here on Earth in the past year, when nobody knew from day to day if the boycott was going to work and whether or not people could get to their jobs.

The time for sorrow was past—thank you, Jesus. Mahalia worked the audience into a bounce with "How I Got Over." Negroes hadn't ridden buses in a year and still they had made it to work! Most of them had held on to their jobs! And they had run the bus company into the ground! Carried along by Mildred's toe-tapping tempo, clapping her hands here and there in unexpected places as the beat got stronger and stronger, moving with grace despite her heaviness, Mahalia sang on and on, verse after verse, repeating lines, adding notes, revealing herself: "'I feel like shouting . . . I'm gonna sing and never get ti-red.'"

"Sing the song, girl!" shouted one listener. "Oh yes, Jesus," another cried.

It was time to bring the audience back down to earth. Mahalia chose a quiet hymn, "God Is So Good to Me," that was more prayer than song. "'I know how to pray and always do,'" she sang in a soft, feather-light voice, "'and every time He'll bring me through.'"

Mahalia felt moved to speak: "The Lord has blessed me. I was nothing and He lifted me up. But the success of one Negro doesn't mean anything if every Negro isn't completely free."

The boycott wasn't over yet, and these people needed a song to give them courage to see it through. "'I'm goin' mooove on up a little high-er,'" she began, with her rock-steady sense of pulse. The song was about finding treasures in heaven—"'gonna meet my loving mother . . . gonna drink from the Christian fountain'"—but it could as well have been about striving for treasures here on Earth: a day without humiliation, a seat on a bus. With Mildred pounding out chords like drumbeats, Mahalia swept the people up in her fervor. It became impossible not to move, tap, snap, or clap *something*.

The church rocked.

Finally, she sent everyone home with a solemn "'Si-hi-ilent ni-hi-ieeght,'" unraveling the syllables like thread from a spool, giving Montgomery a holy night to remember.

The hecklers passed the Abernathy house in such a steady stream that night that the noise actually put Mahalia to sleep. In the morning she was relieved to board the train with Mildred and put Montgomery behind her.

But that quiet, well-spoken Reverend—she would gladly do for Martin again. Something he had said stuck in her mind: "God is personal." He had explained to her that during the early weeks of the boycott, he was fearing terribly for his and his family's safety. He heard the voice of Jesus telling him to fight on. At that moment, God became real and personal to him for the first time. Mahalia knew what Martin was talking about, oh yes. Hadn't she been reading her Bible and praying to God each and every day for as long as she could remember? "'Yes, God is real, oh, He's real in my soul,'" she sang softly to herself.

When she got home, Mahalia told her friend Nettie about the brave young preacher she had met. "That Martin, he has a wisdom. I believe he is a black Moses, come to lead his people, and I believe God's going to part the waters."

The waters parted on December 20, 1956, when the Supreme Court order to desegregate the buses reached the city. Early the next morning the Reverends King and Abernathy boarded the first integrated Montgomery City Lines bus. After 381 days, the boycott was over.

Riding the first integrated bus in Montgomery on December 21, 1956: Rev. Ralph Abernathy (front row, on left), Rev. Martin Luther King Jr. (back row, on left), Rev. Glenn Smiley (back row, on right), and an unidentified woman and boy.

Just in time for Christmas. Mahalia celebrated by having three trees. One tree stood in the living room, and two more graced the front yard along with the three wise men and Jesus, Mary, and Joseph on a donkey. Mahalia strung hundreds upon hundreds of lights outside, causing traffic to slow to a standstill nightly as people gawked. Barefoot little Halie, who had never had even one tree in New Orleans, now had three. With lights. In a home of her own. She wandered in and out of rooms, singing.

How nice it was—thank you, Lord—to come home to a beautiful house fixed just the way she liked. But each time she put her key in the door, there was nobody to greet her in the hall.

Mahalia was lonesome.

Romantic Interlude: Russell

What about the Reverend Russell Roberts of Atlantic City? He sure was one good-looking man. Tall, with smooth skin and a tidy little mustache. A great preacher, and educated, but he liked to joke, too. He came from Massachusetts: a Yankee with a southern girl, ooooh!

They had met in 1954 while working together on a fundraiser for two Chicago youth groups. They were seen together—and gossiped about—at the next National Baptist Convention. He came to New York City to listen in while she made a recording. She stopped in Atlantic City to visit. Things had become serious by 1956, but Mahalia was cautious. She had made a mistake the first time, with Ike, and she didn't want to make another.

She confided in her friend Celeste Scott: "Thing is, I'm wondering if he loves me or Mahalia Jackson?"

"Mahalia, you're the only one can answer that. That, and how do you feel about *him*," said Celeste.

Mildred thought they made a beautiful team in the pulpit in Atlantic City. Mahalia seemed to know just the right songs to prepare the way for Russell's preaching. But he was too high-minded for down-to-earth Mahalia, Mildred thought. "I just don't think he's for you," she told Mahalia. Mahalia exploded, and Mildred bit her tongue forever after on *that* subject.

By the following spring, Mahalia felt ready for marriage. But she was anxious and having trouble breathing again. She went to see Dr. Barclay, who said the problem was sarcoid disease in her lungs and being overweight. He prescribed the drug prednisone, which increased her appetite, and at the same time, he told her to lose a lot of weight. They argued. "If I lose all you want me to lose, people won't

Mahalia performing at the Newport Jazz Festival during the time of her courtship with Russell Roberts.

think I'm Mahalia Jackson, and *I* won't think I'm Mahalia Jackson." To her, being heavy was a sign of success and health. The days of State Street chicken were over; she could have ribs any time she wanted. Or heaps of fried chicken. Or steak.

Besides, Russell didn't think she was too heavy. Else why would he ask her to marry him? Mahalia said yes. They talked about a wedding and a honeymoon in Europe. Then Russell got sick. Cancer. He took treatments, and she prayed, alone in the night: "Take his hand, precious Lord."

Russell Roberts.

But Russell got worse, not better. Mahalia, desperate, sandwiched a quick trip to Atlantic City into her schedule. She pulled ten thousand dollars from her purse and gave it to Russell. "What can I do? Besides giving you this for the best treatment in the country. What can I do?" She went home with a record he had made of his preaching, and a heavy heart.

Early one February morning, 1959, she got a telephone call: Russell was dead. That night, she sang a big concert in Chicago's Orchestra Hall, but at two o'clock in the morning she called her friend Nettie, sobbing, asking her to come and stay with her. Light candles next to Russell's photograph in a frame, set in the pink bedroom next to her bedroom. Pace, pray, play the record he gave her. "I feel his presence so close," she told Nettie. "Russell is here, and I don't know what he's trying to tell me."

Mahalia continued to feel lonely and distraught for months, especially at night. She'd phone Nettie—"I can't sleep; I wish you'd come down here"—and her warm-hearted friend came. Night after night Mahalia lit the candles and played the record until at last she knew what Russell was trying to tell her. He loved her, truly. She kept his photograph on her dresser for the rest of her life.

Battle in the Studio

Mahalia was pleased with the new producer at Columbia Records, Irving Townsend. So pale, slim, and young, he seemed different from other recording men. He actually said she could sing what she wanted. "I feel you should do—and can be doing—the kinds of things that are closest to you, Mahalia, that you know best, and love, and have grown up with."

Could it be true? Goodbye, "A Rusty Old Halo." Hello, "Didn't It Rain," "My God Is Real (Yes, God Is Real)," and "His Eye Is on the Sparrow." Townsend wanted her to sing some new things, too. Well, all right. A suite for orchestra called *Black, Brown, and Beige*, by Duke Ellington. She balked. Duke was jazz and Mahalia Jackson didn't sing jazz, remember?

"*Black, Brown, and Beige* tells the whole history of the Negro people in music, but all you record is the religious part, 'Come Sunday,' see?" Townsend said.

Duke Ellington working with Mahalia.

"I can't record with no orchestra. I can't read a—"

"I know you can't read music, Mahalia. Just learn it. It isn't long. He's changing the whole damned thing, just to fit you in."

She would have every preacher in the National Baptist Convention on her back when they saw her name on a record of Duke's. She said no. They argued, and Townsend lost his temper. "If I have to drag you kicking and screaming, you're going to do it. It's for your own good!" he shouted.

Ellington, when he heard of the battle, called Mahalia. "Doll, it's a breeze," he said in his soft, charming voice. He always dressed so nice, in a fine suit, with a silk handkerchief in the pocket. He had been to her home and enjoyed her food. Man knew how to eat: gumbo and rice, chicken, steak, ham hocks and greens, corn bread, salad, cake and pie! Afterward, he played the piano and she sang. That man, he was the daddy of them all.

Call Mildred. Get Eliot Beal, choral director and an old friend from New Orleans, to teach her the part note by note. Rehearse,

rehearse, then rehearse some more. Mahalia, who never sang a song as it was written and never ever the same way twice, tried to wrestle with music that had no room for alterations. Past midnight and into the morning she was to leave they worked, and still Mahalia didn't have it. She boarded the train for Los Angeles, protesting.

In Duke's hotel suite, he tried to get her to pronounce the words correctly. Nothing new there. Every time she made a record, somebody pestered her about the way she sang words.

"You all trying to make me an opera singer," she complained as they walked into the Columbia studios on Sunset Boulevard. She got through "Come Sunday" all right, and even hummed an extra chorus. Then Duke asked her to sing the Twenty-third Psalm.

Mahalia was quiet. "I don't know nothing about that," she said warily. She had had trouble enough preparing "Come Sunday." Nobody had said anything to her about any psalm.

Duke struck a chord on the piano, opening a door, beckoning. "Open your Bible and sing, woman!"

"'Th' Lord is my shepherd, I shall not want,'" she began, her voice strong and dark. With Mahalia leading the way and Duke following, bringing the orchestra in and out, they improvised. "'He leadeth me,'" her voice took a graceful, daring leap up the scale, and the horns fell silent. She finished with an *Ah-mayn* that was high and mighty, and Duke brought the full orchestra in to cradle the sound. The clarinetist delivered a brief melodic flourish like a graceful curtsy, and the psalm was over.

Mahalia took a deep breath of relief and said, "Duke, you a terrible man."

"And you," she said, turning to Townsend, "you made me do it."

"Mahalia, nobody can make you do anything you don't want to do," he replied.

Holiday

Think of it: Jesus Christ was baptized less than a mile from here, in water that flowed by this exact spot. Mahalia cupped her hands and drew up a handful of the Jordan River. It was as muddy as the Mississippi, where she was baptized at age fifteen in a long white cotton batiste gown. She let the cool water run through her long fingers, remembering what the Bible said: "And Jesus, when he was baptized, went up straightaway out of the water: and, lo, the heavens were opened unto him, and he saw the Spirit of God descending like a dove. . . ."

She was finally taking her trip through the Holy Land, in 1961. With only one concert to give, in Tel Aviv, she was free to walk and look and wonder for two weeks. She would see the places she had been reading about all her life in the Bible.

Making the pilgrimage with her were Mildred, a publicity man, a woman journalist, and David Haber, her road manager. They all

Jerusalem at last. Mahalia made her pilgrimage to the Holy Land in 1961.

squeezed into a car driven by a tall, imposing Arab whom Mahalia nicknamed Fez as soon as she learned the name of the little red hat he wore.

Outside Jericho, Fez showed Mahalia the spot where the ancient walls once stood. Here Joshua gave the order to the Israelites to shout when they heard a long blast from the trumpets. "'And the walls come a-tumbling down . . . ,'" Mahalia sang with her eyes shining. Turning to Haber she said, with a smile that lit up her face, "Oh, Dave-honey, isn't it wonderful?"

He looked at her curiously. To many people, the battle at Jericho was a story in a book. Here was a woman overcome with delight at the sight of, well, nothing you could see, not now, anyway.

"Mahalia, do you believe Joshua actually brought the walls down with trumpets?" he asked.

"I believe Joshua did pray to God, and the sun stood still," she said, standing tall. "I believe everything." Every page in the Bible was real, to her.

The road from Jericho to Jerusalem was a twisting, up-and-down, dirt-blown pass through rocky hills, which Fez took at a speed more suitable to a four-lane highway stretching across the Great Plains. Mahalia became so frightened she could hardly breathe. A voice spoke to her: "If Joseph could bring Mary over these mountains on a donkey, why do you fear?" She calmed down at once. "I'm sorry, Lord," she murmured.

They stopped in Bethlehem, where a guide led Mahalia to a church that was built above Christ's birthplace. Down, down steep steps she descended to a tiny chapel lit by hanging candles. A silver star in the floor marked the very spot: "Here Jesus Christ was born of the Virgin Mary" the inscription read, in Latin. Mahalia knelt and prayed. "For unto you is born in the city of David a Savior, which is Christ the Lord."

Mahalia roamed alone through the sweet-smelling garden of Gethsemane. How could Christ have suffered in such a beautiful place? But look: the old, old olive trees. Their trunks, so thick and gnarled and twisted, tell the story of agony. Among these very trees Judas betrayed Jesus with a kiss. "Don't you feel it?" she asked Dave in a quiet voice.

Jerusalem at last. Mahalia rested briefly in the pension owned by a warm, welcoming Arab woman. Then she put on her most comfortable shoes, her beaded moccasins, and took up her walking stick, humming. Halie was going to walk up to Calvary. She was going to trudge the path that Jesus trudged to his death.

The path was more like an alley, with high stone walls on either side. The mournful wail of Arab music trailed her at every turn, past postcard shops and up stairs. Here Jesus took up the cross and the crown of thorns, his ears ringing with mocking cries. There Jesus fell under his cross. The air was close and hot, and Mahalia's dress clung damply to her back. Here Jesus said to the women who were following him, "Weep not for me, but weep for yourselves, and your children." The steps seemed endless, and Mahalia, who was at her heaviest weight, 240 pounds, was panting a lot. "When we going start up to Calvary?" she asked the guide.

"We're on Calvary now."

"Oh!" said Mahalia, embarrassed. She had been expecting a rocky promontory shaped like a skull, the Golgotha of the Bible. Instead the guide pointed to an arched doorway, and Mahalia entered a vast, multichambered basilica, the Church of the Holy Sepulcher.

Up a steep staircase to a small chapel within, and Mahalia found it: the place where the cross stood. "And it was the third hour, and they crucified him." Mahalia put her hand inside a hole surrounded by a silver circle, and felt the very rock. Think of it!

Padding softly through the basilica, Mahalia came to the rotunda and stooped to enter through a low door. There, under a marble bench, was the exact stone slab where a rich man, Joseph of Arimathea, laid Jesus' body in preparation for burial. "And he bought fine linen, and took him down, and wrapped him in the linen, and laid him in a sepulcher which was hewn out of a rock, and rolled a stone unto the door of the sepulcher." On a nearby pedestal stood a piece of the very stone that sealed Jesus in his grave—and three days later was found rolled back, with Jesus gone.

Mahalia sank to her knees. She, Halie Jackson, was a living witness to all she had been singing about for forty-five years. Glory to the Lord.

The Great March

More and more, the Lord's business seemed tied up with civil rights business. By 1963 it was impossible to separate the two; gospel songs and spirituals propelled the marches, prolonged the sit-ins, and drove the freedom rides. Mahalia lent her voice to the demonstrations whenever she was asked. How could she not say yes? In Birmingham, Alabama, firemen and police turned powerful hoses and snarling dogs on children—children!—who were marching for the right to play in the same parks and use the same drinking fountains as whites.

When Dr. Martin Luther King Jr. needed bail money for his demonstrators in Birmingham, Mahalia went straight to Mayor Daley. He gave her the five-thousand-seat Arie Crown Theater and all the police support she needed, for free. She put on a program with Dr. King as speaker and Aretha Franklin rocking the place out with her "Take My Hand, Precious Lord," and when the night was over,

Mahalia had raised fifty thousand dollars for Martin's protest.

Now this march. A. Philip Randolph, the Negro labor leader, was going to hold a massive march in Washington, D.C., on August 28, 1963. President John F. Kennedy had tried to block the march because he was afraid it would bring violence to the capital. But when he considered how one hundred thousand Negroes walking down Constitution Avenue could help persuade Congress to pass his civil rights bill, he changed his mind. The bill said that Negroes could use any restroom, eat in any restaurant, stay in any hotel, and go to any school they wanted. Martin was going to march, and Ralph Abernathy and every other Negro leader, political or religious, and of course Mahalia wanted to be there, too.

For an event of such magnitude, she would need a new hat. Call Ida in New Orleans. Nobody made hats like her old friend Ida Beal, and Ida got things done.

"*Mm-mmh*, that look good," said Mahalia, putting on the creation Ida had brought with her to Chicago, a small, tall hat of purple and brown chiffon leaves with berries hidden among them.

"If they have any kind of breeze at all, those berries will show," said Ida. "Just be sure you pin it good. You know how you are." Mahalia had a habit of shaking her head and sending hair and hatpins flying when she sang.

"Washington going know what I mean when I say I got a friend in New Orleans can beat all those hats in New York!"

Mahalia arrived in the nation's capital on the evening of Tuesday, August 27, to find a city prepared for war. The residents, fearing riots, had fled. Storeowners afraid of looting had closed up shop and sent their goods back to the warehouse. The baseball team, the Washington Senators, had postponed its games until after the march. Police were everywhere.

Mahalia got up early the next morning and dressed in a smart suit and pinned a large corsage to the jacket. To save her breath, she proceeded straight to the end point, the Lincoln Memorial, and settled in her place on the speakers' platform to watch the great march unfold. The weather was pleasantly warm, instead of the usual hot and sticky weather that was typical for Washington in August. There was just enough of a breeze to flutter the leaves on the new hat.

Around noon, she saw the first marchers begin to pour from Constitution Avenue onto the acres of grass surrounding the Lincoln Memorial. They waved signs that read: WE SEEK THE FREEDOM IN 1963 PROMISED IN 1863! and WE DEMAND EQUAL RIGHTS NOW and LOOK MOM! DOGS HAVE TV SHOWS! NEGROES DON'T! It was true; a dog named Lassie had her own television show, but no colored people did. The marchers sang the anthems of the movement: "Fre-e-e-dom, fre-e-e-dom . . ." and "We shall overco-o-ome. . . . Deep in our hea-a-arts we do believe that we shall overcome one day."

On and on they came, the walking people. Mr. Randolph had said he could get one hundred thousand marchers, but this looked like more. They were colored *and* white, city folk and poor farmers, mostly dressed in their Sunday best but not all—plenty of students in blue jeans, too. Wave after wave of people. Some cooled their feet in the long, rectangular reflecting pool. Others spread out blankets and opened baskets as if they were on a Sunday picnic. Mahalia saw a white man help a colored woman who was struggling to march with four children. He picked up one of the kids, and they all walked on together. Such fellowship. So much love. It was as if all members of the human race had taken a day off from being mean to each other.

Around her the platform filled with movement leaders. Mr. Randolph took a seat, and Roy Wilkins, head of the National Association for the Advancement of Colored People. John Lewis, chairman of the Student Nonviolent Coordinating Committee, who had been jailed and beaten more times than maybe even he could count, and he just twenty-three, was there. And of course the ministers, so often the quiet, driving forces behind the movement, and the not-so-quiet driver of them all, Martin, and his right-hand man, Ralph. Soon the dignitaries were packed folding chair to folding chair, knees to backs.

As Mr. Randolph began to speak, saying, "We are gathered here in the largest demonstration in the history of the nation . . . ," Mahalia looked across the flat expanse of parkland, toward the Washington monument. It was people as far as she could see. When had so many Negroes gathered for their own cause? When had so many white people gathered for colored people? Mahalia felt a tug at her heart that made her want to *sing*. But she had to wait past speaker after speaker, until her turn came.

Mahalia was among the 250,000 who assembled in Washington, D.C., on August 28, 1963, to march for equal rights.

It was nearly three o'clock when Mahalia stood. By then the marchers were restless and sun-weary. Some were leaving. She leaned toward Martin, who often had a suggestion for a song. He wanted "I've Been 'Buked."

"'I been 'buked, and I been scorned,'" she began singing slowly into a fleet of microphones. At the sound of the old, favorite spiritual,

*Marchers in front of the
Lincoln Memorial.*

the vast crowd grew still, and the people who were leaving changed
their minds. "'I'm gonna tell my Lord when I get home, how you been
mistreatin' me so long.'" Mahalia sang and hummed, improvising now,
with Mildred keeping pace on the organ. A great murmur came rolling
back to her from the multitude. She had reached them, the walking
people. She had touched their hearts where it hurt. "'Ain't goin' to lay
my religion down, no, Lord,'" she sang, and erased the fatigue of this
long, important day. "Hallelujah!" she shouted.

Picking up the tempo, Mildred launched into another song,
"Stand By Me," and Mahalia felt herself getting warmed up as she reg-
istered the crowd's responses, the *amen*s and *all right*s! There were cries
of "More, more, more!" and she did not deny the requests but broke
right into the fast, foot-stomping "How I Got Over." The line about
thanking God for old-time religion brought an extra measure of

Hallelujahs from people who knew how to hold on to their religion in times of trial. Hallelujah!

Mahalia, panting and perspiring, sat down at last.

Hallelujah, indeed. The mustard seed was a sturdy tree. In Montgomery and other places, she had sung out her protest, not in freedom songs but in God's songs, and people had listened. Tens upon thousands had listened this time. The birds of the air had come: the marching people! They had made nests in the branches of her tree! Listening to her songs, they had found a place to rest and gather strength for the struggle ahead.

At last it was time for Mr. Randolph to introduce Dr. Martin Luther King Jr., "the *moral* leader of the nation." Martin rose. A roar went up from the crowd. He began, "I am happy to join with you today in what will go down in history as the greatest demonstration

Mahalia singing at the March on Washington, with Dr. Martin Luther King Jr. listening at bottom right and his wife, Coretta Scott King, sitting nearby (in sunglasses).

Dr. Martin Luther King Jr. waving to the crowd during the Great March.

for freedom in the history of our nation. . . ." He followed his carefully prepared speech until, looking up suddenly from the paper, he began to improvise, from the heart. His friends sitting nearby encouraged him: "Tell it, doctor!" "Awright!"

Mahalia leaned forward and whispered, "Tell them about the dream, Martin."

He had spoken about his "dream" before; lately it had been one of his favorite themes. "I have a dream," he began, as people listening just below him joined hands and swayed back and forth, shouting, urging him on, as if they were in church. "I have a dream that my four little children will one day live in a nation where they will not be judged by the color of their skin but by the content of their character.

I have a dream today. . . ." Reverend King preached as he had never preached before, to the largest congregation in the world. Finished, he stepped back, dripping sweat, as another roar swept the park.

Mahalia lay with her Bible a long time that night, thinking over the great day's events. The March on Washington for Jobs and Freedom had been the largest civil rights demonstration in history, Walter Cronkite said on the TV news. It had drawn not 100,000 people, as the organizers had expected, but 250,000. Sixty thousand of the marchers were white.

Imagine: all those people wanting freedom for her people. And not a single rock thrown.

ALAMEDA FREE LIBRARY

"Everybody Need Somebody"

Everyone said Mahalia's house was like Grand Central Station, and Mahalia liked it that way. People were always filing through: gospel singers and players; her agent; her lawyer; the Bronzeville reverends who came to lay their church problems at her feet; Ike, asking for a "loan" (and always getting one); and cousins, aunts, uncles, and friends visiting from New Orleans and other places.

A person could get lonesome, though, with so many people around. She wouldn't tell it to just anyone, but she could talk to Cousin Celie.

"Sometimes I get lonely, Celie," she said on the telephone. "There is so much on me, and I don't have nobody. Even Adam, when the Lord saw he was lonely, He gave him a companion. I feel like I would like companionship, someone that really cares."

"If you should, I wouldn't dare be against it," Celie said. "I would shout for joy."

They chatted on. Aunt Bell's diabetes was so bad she could lose a leg. Poor Aunt Bell. Mahalia would have to do something nice for her. It was Bell who predicted that little Halie would grow up to be famous and walk with kings and queens. But no one in the Clark family, and Mahalia least of all, could have predicted, back when she was keeping one eye on Brisko and the other on shelling peas, what it would be like to have millions of people loving you but still feel alone.

"Celie, this prestige mess is nothing," Mahalia said, and hung up the phone. She looked at Russell's picture and went to put his record on the phonograph.

Mahalia decided to give her aunt the biggest birthday she'd ever had. And so Aunt Bell turned eighty-five with one leg gone but her little house in New Orleans full of family and friends from as far away as New York.

Bell sat on her bed in a blue gown, her hair tied with a blue satin ribbon. Her granddaughter draped a mink stole around her shoulders. Celie marched in with a big cake, singing "Happy Birthday," and Mahalia took pictures with her new color movie camera.

It was nearly midnight when Mahalia rose from her aunt's bedside to give her some rest. Bell called after her in a clear voice, "Baby?"

"Yes?" said Mahalia, stopping.

"Auntie want to tell you something."

When Bell spoke, Mahalia listened, because Aunt Bell had second sight. Mahalia sat down on the bed.

"I see something set ahead of you, and if you don't be very particular, you're going to fall into it, and it's not going to be so easy to unwind out of," Bell said in a low voice. "I want you to be very particular. And remember all I said."

Bell died one month later, on January 27, 1964.

Mahalia took charge of the funeral, from the food to the casket to the music; choosing the minister and the flowers—which she did herself after she couldn't find a florist in New Orleans to carry out her designs. At the wake Aunt Duke, now frail, took one look at her sister's body and fled to the porch to moan without cease, "I want to go where my sister Bell, I want to go-o-o-o where. . . ."

Mahalia, usually restrained at funerals, let herself go. This time it was Aunt Bell who had departed—Aunt Bell, who had nursed little Halie and defended her against the rages of Aunt Duke, saying: "Whip her next time, sister, not this time!" Grief took hold of Mahalia, and sent her into a frenzy, shouting and sobbing. She fell out, she collapsed in a faint. It took several ushers in white dresses and caps, always on hand to minister to those who were overcome at church services, to bring Mahalia back to this earth with fans and smelling salts.

Aunt Bell's passing left a hole. Mahalia felt it most keenly whenever she returned from one of her many trips away. "Everybody need somebody," she told her friend Nettie.

Romantic Interlude: Minters

There was a man—a considerate man who came from a good family in nearby Gary, Indiana. Sigmond Galloway, called Minters or Minnis, had been seeing Mahalia casually for more than a year. He was seven years younger than she—forty-five to her fifty-two years—light skinned, with a neat little mustache and bushy eyebrows, and he dressed sharp. He looked a lot like Russell, in fact. He was Baptist, like her, a widower with a five-year-old girl named Sigma. Mahalia, who couldn't have children, loved the sturdy little girl. And Minters—he was the politest escort she had ever had.

His family had a construction business, but he worked as a musician, playing saxophone and flute, mostly in recording studios but also in clubs. A jazzman. Well, that's all right. She didn't have to go to the clubs, did she. Should she marry him if he asked?

Anxiously she polled her friends. Polly, her secretary, said no. Reverend Leon Jenkins, her pastor, from Greater Salem Baptist

Mahalia and Minters Sigmond Galloway on their wedding day in Chicago in 1964.

Church: Yes. Mildred: No. Mahalia's doubts rose and fell. Dr. Barclay: No. (He saw her as a sick woman in need of large amounts of love and care, and Minters as the wrong man for the job.) Lou Mindling, her manager: No. Gwen Lightner, a friend from early gospel days in Chicago said, "Ask God to direct you."

God directed her to say yes. And so, on a July morning in 1964, Reverend Jenkins, Reverend John Thurston (who was another pastor-friend), and Minters assembled in her living room. Upstairs Mahalia put on a blue dress and pinned on a corsage, with Polly's help. Still, Mahalia was unsure. "There's a burden around my heart," she told Polly. Then: "No, I'll go on."

Reverend Jenkins performed the simple ceremony, and seven minutes later Mahalia was Mrs. Sigmond Galloway.

A press reception followed atop the Prudential Building in downtown Chicago: champagne, flash bulbs, and dinner. Minters glowed in the spotlight of attention accorded a star. Mahalia glowed in his little attentions: a kiss on the cheek, a hand on her elbow to guide her.

A few months later, when *Ebony* magazine came for an interview, she showed off her husband and her house with its new two-story addition and lacy, white iron balcony like the rich folks had in New Orleans, telling the reporter proudly: "For twenty-one years, I came home from long tours to an empty house. Now someone waits for me."

Be Very Particular

Just who *had* she married? Mahalia began to wonder. Minters brought out the whisky every time someone came to the house, and people came in a steady stream. Mahalia had a rule against serving liquor, out of respect for the ministers who were nearly always present. Minters paid no attention.

When they went to New York City he insisted on sitting in on her interviews and correcting her speech, embarrassing her in front of the press people. At night he made the rounds of the jazz clubs, leaving her in their hotel room, wondering where that polite escort, so willing to do for *her,* had gone.

She thought she was getting a companion who would smooth the way in her turbulent life. *He* thought he was getting a guide to a glamorous world that he wouldn't be able to enter otherwise. They were both disappointed.

Three months after their wedding, Mahalia went into the hospital. Her heart beat too fast, she was short of breath, and she had other troubles no doctor could name.

Nursemaid was the last thing Minters wanted to be. He was all set to meet people and go places, and invitations were pouring in, too. There was even one from President Lyndon B. Johnson, inviting Mahalia to the White House for his inauguration. For Minters it was the last straw.

"Come on, get up from there!" he shouted. "I'm not going to let you pass this up, you hear me? You can just stop acting like a child. There's nothing the matter with you."

Mahalia could not get out of bed. Minters went to the inauguration alone.

She had visions of a coffin closing over her head. Celie, come for a long visit, said it was not so. Jesus had spoken to Celie. "He's going to let you get up, and you're going to sing better than ever," she said.

"You think so?" Mahalia asked with tears in her eyes.

"I know so."

Still Mahalia could not get well.

One day in July 1965 Minters came home and said, "Hey, what are you doing in that bed? Get on up!"

"Minters, don't start that mess. I'm sick," she replied.

"Oh, nothing wrong with you!" he said, and kissed her on the cheek. He had made a reservation at the Sheraton Hotel's elegant Kon-tiki restaurant for the following night, their first wedding anniversary.

Maybe his enthusiasm was catching, because Mahalia felt well enough the next day to celebrate with a few friends and enjoy the fine seafood. But then Minters had to go and spoil things when he told a member of the hotel staff, "This is Mahalia Jackson. Go get her car."

She never liked it when people fussed over her because she was famous. "Minnis, you get the car," she said quietly. She waited until they were settled inside to say, "Don't go telling people I'm Mahalia Jackson. I don't need people making over me."

"Well, you're the queen," Minters said. "I want the best for you!"

The best for her or the best for Sigmond Galloway? Aunt Bell had seen it coming: something Mahalia was going to fall into. "Be very particular." Mahalia had not seen it coming, and now she was sitting in it: marriage to the wrong man, again. Where was the man who would love *her*, not Mahalia Jackson?

Thanksgiving 1966: Minters's mother cooked the turkey, and Mahalia prepared the rest. Always plenty food at Mahalia's; company, too. For once Mahalia didn't object to Minters serving liquor, and he was generous!

The party rolled happily on until it was time to take Minters's mother and Sigma home, and Mahalia looked around for her husband. He was gone. Vanished. She made some phone calls and located him. "Get back here and see to your mother and child!" she shouted into the telephone. Minters returned and drove them home, but when he came back, he unleashed his fury upon Mahalia. He swung at her and missed, smashing his hand into the dresser. He fled to the hospital emergency room. She fled to a hotel, and then to Aunt Hannah's.

Minters refused to budge from their house, and Mahalia refused to enter with him in it. She filed for divorce. The marriage had lasted less than two and a half years.

Hollis Studio

Late Years

1967—1972

Carry On

It was a messy divorce, what with Minters fighting for alimony and Mahalia fighting for the house. She was still a sick woman, in bed more than she was out. Yet she carried on—and was tremendous.

On Easter Sunday 1967, in New York's Philharmonic Hall, she mustered "an easy, perfectly controlled contralto that can move without a misstep from a fluttering falsetto to a low, embracing moan," said critic Whitney Balliett in the *New Yorker* magazine. How did Mahalia do it? How did she keep on keeping on when she felt so bad? Sheer will. And something more. "It was nothing but the hand of God," she told her audience in New York. "I'm the instrument." Mahalia was able to go out and sing for three hours straight twice in one day because she had been called to do so. She believed.

She was no longer just a gospel singer. Mahalia was a famous entertainer singing the good news all around the world. Oh, she still made time for church dates (and never missed a revival at Greater Salem Baptist), because church was home. Church had taken her in when her heart ached from knowing her mother was far away in Heaven, and many times since. Church would always be home. But Mahalia also kept in mind what Jesus said: "These things I do and greater things will you do." She had a responsibility to use the gift God gave her. She had to do greater things.

Sometimes, though, the responsibility was too much. Mahalia started off on a long tour of Europe—and couldn't get past the first stop, Berlin. Her heart started pounding, and she grew frightened. She canceled the tour and flew back to Chicago and Dr. Barclay, who put her in the hospital immediately.

Fierce, protective Polly Fletcher, Mahalia's loyal secretary, put up a sign on Mahalia's hospital door that said NO VISITORS, but Missie Wilkerson went in, anyway, with her pots and pans. Polly was about to put Mahalia's old friend out, but a weak voice said, "Let her in." Mahalia *would* have her way.

Missie set down pots and lifted lids, revealing food that definitely was not what the doctor ordered: ham hocks and greens.

"She can't eat that," Polly snapped.

Mahalia sat up. "Yes, I can," she said. "She brought it. I want it. I'm going eat it." Good Louisiana cooking—mixed with prayer—had straightened Halie's fishhook legs; it could make her heart strong, too.

When Mahalia went home, Polly kept visitors to a bare minimum so she could rest and think about her affairs. "I'm going clean me a few plates," she told Celie on the telephone.

Mahalia carrying on in later life.

First, let her manager, Lou Mindling, go. Next, hire a new manager, someone who could get her more money for her concerts and more work on television, so she wouldn't have to travel so much. She called Louis Armstrong's managers, Joe Glaser and his associate Bob Phillips at Associated Booking. They were pleased to take her on, whenever she was ready to sing again.

Sorrow Song

She was ready to sing, if Dr. King was doing the asking. He was leading a strike by black garbage men in Memphis, Tennessee, and he had invited Mahalia to sing. Of course she would, for Martin; the ground that man walked on was holy.

The day before she was to be in Memphis, she turned on the television and got a shock. Martin, shot! She prayed it wasn't as bad as the TV people were making out.

Dead, they said. Mahalia crumpled to the floor. "Oh, my God, Martin—Martin!"

He had been killed by a gunman as he stood on the balcony of his hotel in Memphis on Thursday, April 4, 1968.

How many times had Martin sat at her table and filled his belly with her down-home food, and afterward, sung with her around the piano? How many times had she sung at his mass meetings and demonstrations? He was a black Moses, come to lead his people, and he *had* led them. But the struggle was not over, and now he was—she could hardly bear the thought—gone. "What shall I do? What shall I do?" she wailed as she watched the TV news, sobbing.

In an instant, she knew. Get a friend to drive her to Atlanta to be at Martin's own church, the red brick Ebenezer Baptist, on Sunday morning. Sit with his mother in the front-row pew. Listen to his father, Daddy King, preach: "You and I know these are serious, bewildering times in which we live, but don't you lose your way and don't you ever let it get so dark that you cannot see a star." Hear his brother A. D. preach an angry sermon. Then stand and sing, alone, "'This troubled world is not my final home. . . .'"—the only way to let the feeling out.

Back at the hotel, a meal arrived as if from nowhere—turnip greens, ham, tomatoes, corn sticks, everything she could want—with a box of roses. The card said simply "Coretta King"—Martin's widow.

The funeral, on Tuesday, began at Ebenezer Church, which could hold 750 people. Another 60,000 mourners surrounded the building, listening via loudspeakers. Mahalia, gray-faced and sickly, sat as an invited guest near the pulpit, amid a flock of ministers. A tape was played of the last sermon that Dr. King had preached there. "If any of you are around when I have to meet my day, I don't want a long funeral," said the familiar, melodious voice.

His wishes were disobeyed. The funeral and burial services lasted seven and a half hours.

A faded green farm cart drawn by two mules, symbolizing Dr. King's connection to the poor, carried the casket five miles across the city to Morehouse College, where Dr. King had been a student. Some 50,000 people followed on foot, walking their last walk with their leader, under a broiling sun. Mahalia, feeling too weak for a long, hot march, rode in a car to the second, more public service on the campus lawn.

Short of breath and afraid she wouldn't find her voice, Mahalia found it. The hand of God, again. She sang her sorrow out and delivered a plea for forgiveness: "'Precious Lord, take my hand, lead me on, let me stand. . . .'" It was the song that Martin had requested be played at the Memphis mass meeting to which he was going the night he was killed.

Forgive, if you can. Riots flared in more than a hundred cities, as Negroes destroyed their own neighborhoods as well as white property. The black leader Stokely Carmichael announced, "When white America killed Dr. King, she declared war on us. The only way black people will survive is by getting guns." So they got their guns. Matches, too. In Washington, D.C., more than seven hundred fires lit

Crowds surrounded Dr. Martin Luther King Jr.'s casket as it was drawn through the streets of Atlanta during his funeral.

the sky. A grieving nation responded exactly as Dr. King would *not* have wanted, with violence. In the end, 46 people were dead and 28,000 people were in jail.

Mahalia grieved in the only way she could. She converted the concert she had coming up in Los Angeles with some of gospel's biggest names—James Cleveland, Edwin Hawkins, and the Staple Singers—into a memorial for Martin. At the end Mahalia launched a "We Shall Overcome" that brought the audience out of its seats and up onto the stage in a hollering, jumping mass. The police had to make a path so that Mahalia could get off the stage. She sang all the way to her dressing room, where the other gospel singers crowded in and joined her. The singing continued for another hour and a half. For Martin.

On the Road Again

Christmas 1969: this time one tree would have to do. Mahalia had sold her beloved house after the divorce—place was too full of memories—and she had bought a condominium in a new high-rise building at 5201 South Cornell Avenue. In fact, she had purchased two apartments on the twenty-sixth floor and put them together. Now she had more rooms than she could count and a view of beautiful Lake Michigan, but no yard for her nativity scene.

Good thing she had plenty of company. If there wasn't a traffic jam in her kitchen, it wasn't Christmas. They were eleven at the table, with more to come. Robert Anderson—gospel crooner, songwriter, pianist, and driver of her car over countless miles on the gospel road—knew how to cook a turkey, too. But it was Mahalia's chitlins that everybody was diving into. Even Minters had some. He caught her looking at him and winked.

He had started coming around again. He said he really loved *her*, and not Mahalia Jackson.

She was still sick, off and on. When it was off, she was *on*, singing everywhere. Bermuda. New York. Philadelphia. New Orleans. Portland, Maine. Omaha, Nebraska. Minters accompanied her sometimes. It was nice to have someone to bring her a cup of tea when she was on the road. And he could play flute at her concerts, to give her some rest between songs. If only he weren't so free with her credit cards. Man liked to have a good time—on her nickel. Oh, her eyes were open now; she knew who Sigmond Galloway was and wasn't. She was fifty-eight and lonesome. Everybody need somebody.

The Caribbean. Africa. Japan. India. Her new managers kept her on the road, just like her old managers had. It seemed that nobody could get her the TV work she wanted, aside from guest shots on the variety shows of people like Johnny Cash and Dick Cavett. And so instead of taking it easy, Mahalia was biting off chunks of the world. Lord, give me breath, she prayed.

Intermission in New Delhi, India: Mahalia insisted on changing out of her sweaty dress and into a fresh one, even though she knew the prime minister was waiting. She dabbed a powdered sponge on her forehead, cheeks, and nose, and tidied her shiny black curls. She rose and smoothed the skirt of her long, white chiffon gown. If only her feet didn't hurt so in these tight shoes, she thought as she crossed backstage.

There were others in the room, but Mahalia saw only the slight woman dressed in a simple sari. Prime Minister Indira Gandhi had dark wavy hair with a shock of pale gray rising from her forehead, and her eyes were deep brown and intense. They talked quietly.

"When you coming to America?" Mahalia asked.

"I don't know just yet," Mrs. Gandhi said.

"Well, when you do, you come and stay with me in Chicago."

Mrs. Gandhi nodded, smiling.

It was time for Mahalia to return to the stage, and for the prime minister to head off to a late-night meeting with her cabinet. She was in the middle of a national crisis, watching starving refugees from East Pakistan pour into India at the rate of sixty thousand a day. But as Mrs. Gandhi left, Mahalia's voice, so full of ache and joy and devotion, pulled her back into the auditorium. She canceled her meeting and stood at the fire exit, listening, as the ninety-minute concert stretched to nearly three hours.

Mahalia meeting Prime Minister Indira Gandhi (with U.S. Ambassador Kenneth Keating) in 1971.

The postconcert reception was abuzz with talk of the prime minister's unprecedented behavior, but Mahalia heard none of it. She lay writhing in another room, from pain in her heart. The old pattern had repeated itself: sing for hours with no discomfort, and afterward, collapse. More and more her performances seemed to come from God, and God alone. *How much more work do you have for me, Lord? Halie's feeling tired.*

Celie's Vision

Celie, like her mother, Bell, had second sight, and late in 1971, she saw Mahalia's burials, two of them. One took place "by water" and another "by clay." Birds sang all night long.

Celie didn't say a word to Mahalia, who was in the hospital because of pain in her abdomen. The doctors at Little Company of Mary Hospital, in Evergreen Park, a suburb not far from home, were going to operate on her intestine.

Minters paid her a visit, and so did Aunt Alice and Aunt Hannah, now old and frail. As they gathered their things to go, Mahalia said, "I want you all to kiss me before you leave."

The day before the operation, Mahalia wanted her hair fixed. Her friend Missie came to untangle the braids and comb them out. Mahalia teased, "What are we going to do about Missie?" and Missie teased back, saying she needed a *man*. Laughing like old times.

Mahalia performing near the end of her life.

On Monday, January 24, a doctor performed abdominal surgery on Mahalia. The operation was successful, but the next day her blood pressure began to fall. Early Thursday morning, January 27, 1972, Mahalia Jackson died, alone, of heart failure. She was sixty years old.

Two Funerals

Celie's vision was true enough. Mahalia had two funerals. The grief that poured out for Mahalia was so tremendous that a single service would never have been enough to contain it.

The first funeral was held in Chicago's vast Arie Crown Theater at McCormick Place "by water"—on the shore of Lake Michigan. The second funeral took place "by clay"—the brown soil of Louisiana—in the Rivergate Convention Hall in New Orleans.

In Chicago fifty thousand mourners filed past Mahalia's body, clad in a long blue satin gown and white gloves, as it lay in state at the new, orange-brick Greater Salem Baptist Church on Seventy-first Street and Indiana. A blue cross out front bid EVERYONE WELCOME in neon lights. At the funeral, six thousand people crowded into the Arie Crown Theater, where Coretta King gave thanks for Mahalia's being "black and proud and beautiful," and Aretha Franklin sang "Take My Hand, Precious Lord."

In New Orleans mourners came all night long to view Mahalia's body in the mahogany open casket, her slender hands clutching a Bible. The funeral the next day was long and noisy. Some four thousand people crowded into the convention hall, and another four thousand onlookers pressed against the gates outside, as a local singer sang Mahalia's first hit, "Move On Up a Little Higher," and a chorus of five hundred delivered "I Need Him Every Hour, Most Gracious Lord." On hand were six teams of ushers to help the many mourners who got too high in the spirit and fainted—and the ushers were busy!

The funeral cortege, consisting of the hearse, a white car filled with flowers, and more than twenty-four limousines, snaked its way through the city to Mahalia's old neighborhood. At Mount Moriah Church, where barefoot Halie had scrubbed the floors and found her first solace in singing, loudspeakers set up outside broadcast her songs to the surrounding streets. The cortege continued on to Metairie, a suburb, where Mahalia was buried in Providence Memorial Park in a brief, quiet service.

Her grave lies on a grassy knoll about two blocks from the Mississippi River, where she was baptized. The inscription on her tomb reads: "The world's greatest gospel singer."

Author's Notes

Of Mahalia's many recordings, three were especially representative and thrilling to listen to. *Mahalia Jackson: Gospels, Spirituals & Hymns*, Columbia/Legacy (1991), is a broad sampling of thirty-six songs. *Mahalia Jackson: The Apollo Sessions 1946–1951*, Pair Records (1994), is a selection from Mahalia's early recordings. *Mahalia Jackson: Live at Newport 1958*, Columbia/Legacy (1994), is a solo concert in the Newport Jazz Festival and the closest thing to hearing Mahalia in person. I recommend all of them to the reader.

An exhibition of paintings called "Jacob Lawrence: The Migration Series," at the Museum of Modern Art in 1995, helped me to understand the migration of southern African Americans to northern cities. The paintings are published in *The Great Migration: An American Story/Paintings by Jacob Lawrence*, HarperCollins Children's Books (1993).

The following people and institutions were especially helpful during my research for this book:

John Derbes, former director of Providence Memorial Park, Metairie, Louisiana, set me straight on whether or not Mahalia had a typical New Orleans funeral parade with marching bands and a "second line" of dancing mourners (she did not).

Harold Lucas, executive director of the Black Metropolis Convention & Tourism Council, in Chicago, gave me a personalized tour of the South Side.

Tim Samuelson, curator of architecture at the Chicago Historical Society, corrected the record on several addresses related to Mahalia's private and professional life.

The librarians of the Music Research Division of the New York Public Library for the Performing Arts gave me invaluable assistance, as always.

The congregations of New Hope Baptist Church in Newark, New Jersey, and Pilgrim Baptist Church in Chicago made me feel welcome at their Sunday services.

My thanks to all.

Roxane Orgill

A Select Bibliography

BOOKS

Abernathy, Ralph. *And the Walls Came Tumbling Down*. New York: Harper and Row, 1989.

Drake, St. Clair, and Horace R. Clayton. *Black Metropolis: A Study of Life in a Northern City*. 2 vols. New York: Harper and Row, 1962.

Garrow, David J. *Bearing the Cross: Martin Luther King, Jr., and the Southern Christian Leadership Conference*. New York: William Morrow and Company, Inc., 1986.

Goreau, Laurraine. *Just Mahalia, Baby*. Waco, Texas: Word Books, 1975.

Harris, Michael W. *The Rise of Gospel Blues: The Music of Thomas Andrew Dorsey in the Urban Church*. New York: Oxford University Press, 1992.

Heilbut, Anthony. *The Gospel Sound*. New York: Limelight Editions, 1992.

The Holy Bible. King James Version. Cleveland: World Publishing Company, 1958.

Hull, Mary. *Rosa Parks: Civil Rights Leader*. New York: Chelsea House Publishers, 1994.

Jackson, Mahalia, with Evan McLeod Wylie. *Movin' On Up*. New York: Avon, 1966.

Lemann, Nicholas. *The Promised Land: The Great Black Migration and How It Changed America*. New York: Alfred A. Knopf, 1991.

Lewis, John, with Michael D'Orso. *Walking with the Wind: A Memoir of the Movement*. San Diego: Harcourt Brace and Company, 1998.

National Baptist Convention, U.S.A., ed. *Gospel Pearls*. Nashville: Sunday School Publishing Board, 1921.

Oates, Stephen B. *Let the Trumpet Sound: A Life of Martin Luther King, Jr.* New York: Harper-Collins Publishers, Inc., 1994.

Reese, Della. *Angels Along the Way*. New York: Berkley Publishing Group, 1998.

Schwerin, Jules. *Got To Tell It: Mahalia Jackson, Queen of Gospel*. New York: Oxford University Press, 1992.

Young, Alan. *Woke Me Up This Morning: Black Gospel Singers and the Gospel Life*. Jackson: University Press of Mississippi, 1997.

ARTICLES

Hentoff, Nat. "You Can Still Hear Her Voice When the Music Has Stopped." *Reporter*, 27 June 1957, 34–36.

Jackson, Mahalia. "Bliss vs. Single Blessedness." *Ebony*, April 1968, 89–90, 94–95, 98–100.

Jackson, Mahalia. "To Europe and the Holy Land with Mahalia Jackson." *Ebony*, October 1961, 44–46, 48–50, 53.

Thompson, Era Bell. "Love Comes to Mahalia." *Ebony*, November 1964, 50–60.

von Hoffman, Nicholas. "150,000 Mourn Dr. King in Somber Rites in Atlanta. Mule Wagon Leads March." *Washington Post*, 10 April, 1968.

Index

Photo Credits

Cover image © Bettmann/CORBIS

p.vi   Chicago Historical Society, ICHi-31913

p.xii   Courtesy of John N. Teunisson Photograph Collection, Louisiana Division, New Orleans Public Library

p.3   The Historic New Orleans Collection, accession no. 92-48-L MSS 520 F.858

p.4   The Historic New Orleans Collection, accession no. 1979.325.5738

p.9   George Eastman House/Lewis W. Hine/ Archive Photos

p.12   The Historic New Orleans Collection, accession no. 92-48-L MSS 520 F.864, DETAIL

p.15   Charles L. Franck Photograph, courtesy The Historic New Orleans Collection, Museum/Research Center, accession no. 1974.25.23.97

p.19   Courtesy of the Library of Congress

p.20   Courtesy of the Library of Congress

p.23   Courtesy of the Library of Congress

p.27   Courtesy of the Library of Congress

p.30   Frank Driggs/Archive Photos

p.32   © Bettmann/CORBIS

p.35   Courtesy of Roxane Orgill

p.39   © Jerry Cooke/CORBIS

p.41   A'Lelia Bundles/Walker Family Collection

p.42   Courtesy of the Library of Congress

p.43   Courtesy of Martin and Morris Gospel Sheet Music Collection, Visual and Performing Arts Division, Chicago Public Library

p.44   Hogan Jazz Archive, Howard-Tilton Memorial Library, Tulane University

p.46   © Bettmann/CORBIS

p.47   Left: Hogan Jazz Archive, Howard-Tilton Memorial Library, Tulane University

p.47   Right: Frank Driggs Collection

p.48   Courtesy of Chicago Blues Archives, Visual and Performing Arts Division, Chicago Public Library

p.50   The Historic New Orleans Collection, accession no. 92-48-L MSS 520 F.852

p.53   Tony Vaccaro/Archive Photos

p.55   Archive Photos

p.58   Leonora Shier Collection, Carnegie Hall Archives

p.63   The Historic New Orleans Collection, accession no. 92-48-L MSS 520 F.3286

p.70   Courtesy of Sony Music Photo Library

p.71   Courtesy of the Library of Congress

p.74   Courtesy of Roxane Orgill

p.76   Frank Driggs Collection

p.82   Courtesy of the Library of Congress

p.85   Bob Parent/Archive Photos

p.86   Courtesy of Shiloh Baptist Church, Atlantic City, N.J.

p.88   Frank Driggs Collection

p.91   © Underwood & Underwood/CORBIS

p.97   Archive Photos

p.98   AP/WIDE WORLD PHOTOS

p.99   Bob Parent/Archive Photos

p.100   Archive Photos

p.106   AP/WIDE WORLD PHOTOS

p.110   Courtesy of Bethel New Life Collection, Special Collections and Preservation Division, Chicago Public Library

p.114   Chicago Historical Society, ICHi-31912

p.117   Courtesy of the Library of Congress

p.121   Courtesy Public Affairs, American Embassy, New Delhi

p.123   Chicago Historical Society, ICHi-31914

p.126   Michael P. Smith — www.culturalicons.com

Back cover Bob Parent/Archive Photos

Uncaptioned Photos

p.vi   Mahalia performing in 1970.

p.xii   Cotton on the levee, New Orleans, around 1910.

p.20   A Bronzeville apartment building in 1941.

p.50   Mahalia stopping in New Orleans in 1954.

p.76   Mahalia in her finery.

p.110   Mahalia performing at a ministers' dinner in Chicago in 1967.

p.126   Thomas A. Dorsey visiting Mahalia's grave in 1981.